The Seven Festivals of the Messiah

The Seven Festivals of the Messiah

Edward Chumney

Take note that the name satan and related names are not capitalized. We choose not to acknowledge him, even to the point of violating grammatical rules.

The Hebrew transliterations in this book are provided only where the author felt necessary.

Treasure House

An Imprint of
Destiny Image® Publishers, Inc.
P.O. Box 310
Shippensburg, PA 17257-0310

"For where your treasure is,
there will your heart be also." Matthew 6:21

ISBN 1-56043-767-7

For Worldwide Distribution
Printed in the U.S.A.

Fifth Printing: 2002   Sixth Printing: 2003

This book and all other Destiny Image, Revival Press, MercyPlace, FreshBread, Destiny Image Fiction, and Treasure House books are available at Christian bookstores and distributors worldwide.

For a U.S. bookstore nearest you, call **1-800-722-6774.**
For more information on foreign distributors, call **717-532-3040.**
Or reach us on the Internet:

www.destinyimage.com

Contents

Foreword

The festivals of the L-rd found in the twenty-third chapter of the Book of Leviticus (*Vayikra*) are among the most fascinating and revealing topics of study and inspiration in the entire Bible, yet at the same time, they are probably the least understood. This book will lead you step by step through each festival, examining the foundational truths that G-d wanted us to learn when He gave us these feasts.

Bible believers who are lovers of G-d's Word will discover that the festivals of the L-rd are not only historic events, but are also prophetic. They speak in much detail about the first and second coming of the Messiah (*Mashiach*). In addition, the festivals give us tremendous insight into living the life that G-d desires for us as believers, and into understanding our personal relationship with G-d.

For the Jew, this book will reveal the Messiah (*Mashiach*) in the traditions of the ancient Jewish faith, handed down faithfully from generation to generation. It will answer the question, "Is *Yeshua* [the Hebrew word meaning 'Savior,' translated into English as 'Jesus'], the long-awaited Messiah [*Mashiach*] of Israel?"

Non-Jewish Bible believers will learn to appreciate the Jewish roots of the Christian faith. In addition, ardent Bible prophecy students of both faiths will discover keys of understanding in *The Seven Festivals of the Messiah* to unlock a lot of mystery and confusion in this area.

Regardless of your faith and religious background, I pray that after you read this book and understand the revealing truths G-d laid out in **His** festivals (Leviticus or [*Vayikra*] 23:2,4), you will grow spiritually and your walk with G-d will blossom into a new dimension.

Special Note: I have written this book for both Christian Bible believers and Jewish readers. Both nurture passions for G-d's Word, for His ways, and for His manifestation on earth. Because many Orthodox Jews will be reading this book, I have chosen to honor their fervent commitment to never take G-d's name in vain—even by speaking His Holy Name out loud. Therefore, when I refer directly to the Creator, I will omit certain letters in this manner: G-d or L-rd; or I will use a substitute designation such as "Holy One." I have also tried to retain Hebrew terminology for the festivals and the books of the Tanach or Old Testament for accuracy and to make the content of this book equally palatable for both Jew and Gentile readers. May G-d richly bless you as you seek to learn more about His plan for mankind and our destiny through the seven festivals of the Holy One (blessed be He).

HEBRAIC HERITAGE
MINISTRIES INTERNATIONAL

- Teaching the Hebraic roots of faith in Messiah.
- Networking groups who are studying the Hebraic roots of faith in Messiah.
- Standing with the Jewish people and fighting anti-Semitism.
- Christian Zionists who have a loving heart for the land of Israel.

Please visit our website and join our network!

www.geocities.com/Heartland/2175/index.html

OR

www.hebroots.org

Mailing Address:

Hebraic Heritage Ministries International
P.O. Box 81
Strasburg, Ohio, USA 44680

Chapter 1

The Appointed Feasts

Understanding the Feasts

The festivals of the L-rd found in Leviticus (*Vayikra*) 23 were given to us by G-d so His people could understand the coming of the Messiah (*Mashiach*) and the role that the Messiah (*Mashiach*) would play in redeeming and restoring both man and the earth back to G-d following the fall of man in the Garden of Eden (*Gan Eden*). Although most non-Jewish Bible believers have heard of the feasts, the deep meaning and the importance of these feasts are almost universally not understood.

The apostle Paul (*Rav Sha'ul*) wrote to the Gentile believers in Colossae that the feasts of the L-rd, the new moon, and the Sabbath (*shabbat*) days were *a shadow of things to come* to teach us about the Messiah (*Mashiach*) (Colossians 2:16-17). *Yeshua* (the Hebrew name for Jesus, which means "salvation") was the substance or fulfillment of the greater plan that G-d revealed and foreshadowed in these seven important festivals. To all the readers who are unfamiliar with the festivals, you will be fascinated to discover that the first four feasts or festivals, which are Passover (*Pesach*), Unleavened Bread (*Hag HaMatzah*), First Fruits (*Bikkurim*), and Pentecost (*Shavuot*), primarily teach about the significant events in the first coming of the Messiah (*Mashiach*) and why these events were an important part of G-d's redemption of man. In addition, you will discover that the last three feasts, which are the Feast of Trumpets (*Yom Teruah*; also known as *Rosh HaShanah*), the Day of Atonement (*Yom Kippur*), and the Feast of Booths or Tabernacles (*Sukkot*), give fascinating insight concerning important events that surround the second coming of the Messiah (*Mashiach*).

Why Study the Feasts?

Many non-Jewish Bible believers wonder why they should study and observe the feasts. I believe there are two good reasons. First, although all Bible believers love G-d with all their heart and seek to serve Him daily, most Bible believers do not have an in-depth understanding of the Bible and do not understand the deep depth of the personal relationship that G-d desires us to have with Him. Most Bible believers understand their personal relationship with G-d the same way I viewed my personal relationship with G-d for many, many years: Attend the local congregation of your choice faithfully and regularly, and be a good, moral, honest, and decent person in living your daily life. Because that was all I knew, that was what I accepted. However, G-d began to teach me and show me the deeper things concerning my personal relationship with Him, and a spiritual understanding of the festivals was a big key to unlocking this mystery. If you are a Bible believer and you desire to understand G-d in a greater way than you do today, the festivals will reveal to you the deeper things concerning your personal relationship with Him.

Secondly, the festivals are *G-d's feasts* and *His* appointed times that *we* are to observe (Leviticus [*Vayikra*] 23:1-2,4). G-d gave the festivals to teach about the death, burial, and resurrection of the Messiah (*Mashiach*); the empowering of the believers by the Holy Spirit (*Ruach HaKodesh*); the resurrection of the dead; the coronation of the Messiah; the wedding of the Messiah; the tribulation (*Chevlai shel Mashiach*); the second coming of the Messiah; the millennium (the Messianic age or the *Athid Lavo*); and much, much more.

The Bible provides several powerful reasons for studying and understanding the seven festivals of the Messiah:

1. The feasts are in the Bible, and *all* the Bible is inspired by G-d (2 Timothy 3:16-17).
2. The feasts are a shadow of things to come that teach us about the Messiah (Colossians 2:16-17; Hebrews 10:1).
3. The feasts are prophetic types and examples foreshadowing significant events in G-d's plan of redemption (1 Corinthians 10:1-6,11).
4. G-d gave the feasts so we could learn and understand G-d's plan of redemption for the world and our personal relationship to Him (Romans 15:4).
5. The feasts, as part of the Torah (which means "instruction"), are as a schoolmaster or tutor that leads us to the Messiah (Galatians 3:24).
6. The feasts will point to the Messiah and G-d's plan for the world through the Messiah (Psalm [*Tehillim*] 40:6-8; Hebrews 10:7).

7. *Yeshua* (Jesus) came to fulfill all that was written in the Old Testament (Tanach), which consists of three parts: the Torah, the prophets (*Nevi'im*), and the writings *Ketuvim* (personified by the Psalms) concerning Him (Luke 24:26-27,44-45; John [*Yochanan*] 5:46-47).

8. The feasts set forth the pattern of heavenly things on earth (Hebrews 8:1-2,5; 9:8-9,23; Exodus [*Shemot*] 25:8-9,40; 26:30; Numbers [*Bamidbar*] 8:4; Ezekiel [*Yechezekel*] 43:1-6,10-12).

9. G-d gives the natural to explain the spiritual (1 Corinthians 15:46-47).

10. By studying the natural, we can understand the spiritual (1 Corinthians 2:9-13; 2 Corinthians 4:18).[1]

What Is the Meaning of the Word *Feast* in the Bible?

Two important Hebrew words appear in Leviticus (*Vayikra*) chapter 23, and each word is translated as feast in English. In verse 2, the word for feast is the Hebrew word *mo'ed*, as it is written, "Speak unto the children of Israel, and say unto them, concerning the feasts [*mo'ed*] of the Lord...." The word *mo'ed* means "an appointment, a fixed time or season, a cycle or year, an assembly, an appointed time, a set time or exact time."[2] By understanding the Hebrew meaning of the English word *feast*, we can see that G-d is telling us that *He* is ordaining a "set time or exact time or an appointed time" when He has an appointment with humanity to fulfill certain events in the redemption. In fact, *Yeshua* (Jesus) came to earth at the exact time ordained by G-d (Galatians 4:2,4), and G-d has an exact time or set appointment when, in the future, He will judge the world (Acts 17:31).

In verse 6 is another Hebrew word translated as feast, as it is written, "And on the fifteenth day of the same month is the feast [*chag*] of unleavened bread...." The Hebrew word *chag*, which means a "festival,"[3] is derived from the Hebrew root word *chagag*, which means "to move in a circle, to march in a sacred procession, to celebrate, dance, to hold a solemn feast or holiday."[4] By this we can see that G-d gave the festivals as cycles to be observed yearly so that, by doing them, we can understand G-d's redemptive plan for the world; the role that the Messiah (*Yeshua*) would play in that redemption; and our personal relationship to G-d concerning how we grow from a baby Bible believer to a mature Bible believer. Although G-d gave us the festivals to observe, G-d never gave the festivals so we would obtain salvation from Him by observing them because salvation only comes by faith (*emunah*); however, G-d did give the festivals for the purpose of teaching and instructing His people concerning His plan of redemption and our personal relationship to Him.

The Appointed Place

The feasts are not only G-d's appointed times, but also were to be observed at G-d's appointed place. G-d said that He would choose a place and that it would be a set place where His redemptive plan would be accomplished. Passover (*Pesach*), the Feast of Weeks or Pentecost (*Shavuot*), and the Feast of Tabernacles (*Sukkot*) were to be observed at an appointed place (Deuteronomy [*Devarim*] 16:2,6,9-11, 13-16). This place was Jerusalem (*Yerushalayim*) (2 Kings [*Melachim*] 21:4). From this we can see that Jerusalem (*Yerushalayim*) was appointed by G-d to be the place where important events surrounding the redemptive plan of G-d would be accomplished. *Yeshua* (Jesus) died, was buried, and resurrected in Jerusalem. The empowering of the believers by the Holy Spirit (*Ruach HaKodesh*) took place in

Jerusalem. Messiah (*Yeshua*) will return and set His foot on the Mount of Olives in Jerusalem (Zechariah 14:4) and Jerusalem will be the center of world attention and controversy before the coming of the Messiah (Zechariah 12:2-3; 14:2-4).

Three Times a Year They Were to Assemble

Although there are a total of seven feasts (the divine number for perfection or completeness in the Bible), G-d divided the seven festivals into three major festival seasons. The feasts of Passover (*Pesach*), Unleavened Bread (*Hag HaMatzah*), and First Fruits (*Bikkurim*) are in the Hebrew month of Nisan, which is the first month of G-d's religious calendar in the spring of the year. (We'll examine this calendar a little later.) The Feast of Weeks (*Shavuot*), or Pentecost, is observed in the third month, which is the Hebrew month of Sivan. The Feasts of Trumpets (*Yom Teruah*), Atonement (*Yom Kippur*), and Tabernacles (*Sukkot*) are observed in the seventh month of Tishrei, which is in the fall of the year (Exodus [*Shemot*] 23:14-17; 34:22-23: Deuteronomy [*Devarim*] 16:16-17). Three is the number of complete and perfect testimony and witness (Deuteronomy [*Devarim*] 17:6; 19:15; Matthew [*Mattityahu*] 18:19-20; Luke 24:44-45; 2 Corinthians 13:1; 1 Timothy 5:19; 1 John [*Yochanan*] 5:8). So the feasts are a witness to G-d's divine plan and the role of Messiah (*Yeshua*) fulfilling that plan. This is the message being communicated to Bible believers concerning the three major festival periods in the year.

Traditionally, non-Jewish Bible believers understand the festivals to be exclusively Jewish feasts. However, Leviticus (*Vayikra*) 23:1-2, 4, tells us very clearly that these are *festivals of the L-rd.* In reality, G-d in His divine wisdom instructed us that these festivals are for both Jew and non-Jew, and are to be celebrated jointly with each other (Deuteronomy [*Devarim*] 16:10-11, 14-16). In Deuteronomy (*Devarim*) 16:11, 14, the word translated in English as "stranger" is the Hebrew word *ger*, which means the non-Jew (Bible-believing Gentile) who has joined himself to the Jewish people. Therefore, the L-rd is the Host of the festivals and all Bible believers are His invited guests.

The Biblical Calendar

In order to fully understand and appreciate the feasts being appointed times given by G-d, it is important to understand the biblical calendar that G-d gave us. There are two primary calendars in the Bible. The first is called the civil calendar and is used from Genesis (*Bereishit*) 1:1 to Exodus (*Shemot*) 12. The first month in the civil calendar is Tishrei. *Rosh HaShanah* (the Jewish New Year), the first day in the civil calendar, is the beginning of the new year. The second calendar in the Bible is the religious calendar. The religious calendar is used from Exodus (*Shemot*) 12 to Revelation 22. G-d established the religious calendar in Exodus (*Shemot*) 12:2, as it is written, "This month shall be unto you the beginning of months: it shall be the first month of the year to you." The month that G-d was referring to was the month of Aviv (Exodus 13:4), which is now called the month of Nisan. Prior to G-d's establishing the month of Nisan as the first month in the religious calendar, it was the seventh month in the civil calendar. G-d gave the religious calendar so we could understand that these feasts, which He gave and which are His appointed times and foreshadow important events in the redemption, would happen on the days He ordained on the religious calendar. These important days on the religious calendar are the same days that He gave as festivals in Leviticus (*Vayikra*) 23.

Another understanding for G-d giving a civil calendar and a religious calendar is that everyone who accepts the Messiah (*Yeshua*) into his heart by faith (*emunah*) experiences two birthdays. Just like Tishrei 1 is the first day on the civil calendar and Nisan 1 is the first day on the religious calendar, everyone who accepts the Messiah (*Yeshua*) into his life has a physical (civil) birthday when he was born into the world and a spiritual (religious) birthday the day he accepts the Messiah into his life. The following chart illustrates both types of calendars, showing the names of the months in the biblical calendar.

The Biblical Calendar

Civil Calendar	Religious Calendar
1. Tishrei	1. Nisan (Aviv)
2. Cheshvan	2. Iyar
3. Kislev	3. Sivan
4. Tevet	4. Tammuz
5. Shevat	5. Av
6. Adar	6. Elul
7. Nisan (Aviv)	7. Tishrei
8. Iyar	8. Cheshvan
9. Sivan	9. Kislev
10. Tammuz	10. Tevet
11. Av	11. Shevat
12. Elul	12. Adar

Chapter 2

An Overview of the Festivals

As stated in Chapter 1, the festivals are blueprints through which G-d revealed His overall plan of redemption for both man and the earth following the fall of man in the Garden of Eden (*Gan Eden*) as well as the role that the Messiah (*Yeshua*) would play in that redemption. The festivals are divided into two major portions, depending upon whether they occur in the spring or the fall. The spring festivals teach about the first coming of the Messiah *Yeshua* (Jesus) and the fall festivals teach about the second coming of the Messiah *Yeshua*. In Hosea (*Hoshea*) 6:3 it is written, "...His going forth is prepared as the morning; and He shall come unto us as the rain, as the latter and former rain unto the earth." The "latter and former rain" in this passage is commonly interpreted and understood to be the coming of the Holy Spirit (*Ruach HaKodesh*). This is indeed a valid interpretation and application; however, the former and latter rain also refers to the first and second coming of the Messiah (*Yeshua*).

G-d set up the festivals in an agricultural context. G-d gave the natural for us to understand the spiritual (1 Corinthians 15:46-47). During the course of the year, the rains come in Israel at two primary times—the spring and the fall. If we cross-reference Hosea (*Hoshea*) 6:3 with Joel (*Yoel*) 2:23, we see that the former rain is the Hebrew word *moreh* which means "teacher,"[1] and the word *moderately* in Joel 2:23, is the Hebrew word *tzedakah*, which means "righteousness."[2] The teacher of righteousness was a term for the Messiah. *Yeshua* (Jesus) was the teacher of righteousness sent by G-d as can be seen in John (*Yochanan*) 3:2. *Yeshua* was sent by G-d to the earth to faithfully teach us righteousness, just as G-d faithfully sends us the rain (Isaiah [*Yeshayahu*] 55:10-11). The harvest (believers in the Messiah) is the product that the rain (the Messiah) produces.

In Leviticus 23:2 it is written, "...the feasts of the Lord, which ye shall proclaim to be holy convocations...." The Hebrew term translated as convocation in Leviticus (*Vayikra*) 23:2,4 is *miqra*, which means "a rehearsal."[3] From this we can see that G-d gave the festivals to be yearly "rehearsals" of the future events in the redemption. Because G-d gave the "rehearsals" to teach us about the major events in the redemption, if we want to understand the major events in the redemption, then we need to understand what G-d was teaching us by these rehearsals. The purpose of this book is to show how the "rehearsals" teach us about the real events in the redemption and the role of the Messiah (*Yeshua*) in these events.

In Deuteronomy (*Devarim*) 16:16, G-d instructed the people to come to Jerusalem (*Yerushalayim*) three times a year to observe the feasts. As they came, they observed ceremonies given by G-d that were performed in both the temple (*Beit HaMikdash*) and the home. These ceremonies were twofold in nature. They looked forward and they looked backward. Many of these ceremonies and the specific instructions concerning what was done during these feasts and how they were done can be found in the Mishnah, the oral teaching of Judaism, in the section called Mo'ed. The Mishnah is divided into six orders. Each order is divided into tractates, or different sections of each order. The order called Mo'ed speaks of the festivals. Mo'ed, which we saw earlier means "an appointed time," has two meanings. First, in Deuteronomy (*Devarim*) 16:16, the Jewish people have an appointment to be at a specific place (Jerusalem) at a specific time (the time of the three major pilgrimage festivals). Secondly, G-d has an appointment to perform certain events in the redemption at this time. There are four important aspects to remember when dealing with each of the seven great festivals of the L-rd:

1. All of the festivals are, at the same time, both historical and prophetic.

2. All of the festivals teach about the Messiah (*Yeshua*), or Jesus.

3. All of the festivals are agricultural in context.

4. All of the festivals teach about your personal relationship with G-d and how you are to walk (*halacha*) with Him as you grow in the knowledge of Him, from being a baby believer to a mature believer.

It is important to remember that as an entire unit, the festivals teach and reveal the complete plan of G-d; however, each festival centers on a particular theme in the plan of G-d.

Overview of the Spring Festivals

The four spring festivals are Passover (*Pesach*), Unleavened Bread (*Hag HaMatzah*), First Fruits (*Bikkurim*), and the Feast of Weeks (*Shavuot*), or Pentecost.

1. Passover (*Pesach*) occurs in the first month of the religious calendar (Aviv, also called Nisan), on the fourteenth day, Leviticus (*Vayikra*) 23:5.

2. Unleavened Bread (*Hag HaMatzah*) immediately follows the first day of Passover (*Pesach*). It is observed in the first month (Aviv/Nisan) from the fifteenth day to the twenty-first day (Leviticus [*Vayikra*] 23:6-8).

3. The Feast of First Fruits of the barley harvest (*Bikkurim*) is observed during the week of Unleavened Bread (*Hag HaMatzah*). Anciently, on this day, sheaves of barley were waved before the L-rd in a prescribed ceremony. Today, this festival is not observed in traditional Judaism.

4. The Feast of Weeks (*Shavuot*) is also known as Pentecost. Beginning on the Feast of First Fruits (*Bikkurim*), we begin to count 50 days. This is called the counting of the omer. On the fiftieth day following the Feast of First Fruits (*Bikkurim*) is the Feast of Weeks (*Shavuot*) or Pentecost (Leviticus [*Vayikra*] 23:15-21). (Note: *Pentecost* is a Greek word that literally means "fiftieth.")

These four spring festivals are joined together as an interrelated unit. The Feast of Weeks (*Shavuot*) is considered the conclusion or *atzeret* to Passover. The season of Passover (*Pesach*) is not considered totally over until *Shavuot* (Pentecost) is completed.

The Exodus Story: From *Pesach* to *Shavuot*

Pesach (Passover) begins in Egypt (*Mitzrayim*) (a type of the world), where the children of Israel had become slaves. When the children of Israel cried out to G-d to remember the promises He made to Abraham (*Avraham*), Isaac (*Yitzchak*), and Jacob (*Ya'akov*), G-d called forth a deliverer named Moses (*Moshe*). G-d told Moses (*Moshe*) that He was going to bring the children of Israel out of Egypt (*Mitzrayim*) to the Promised Land (Exodus [*Shemot*] 3:8). When G-d sent Moses (*Moshe*) to Pharaoh, G-d did not tell Moses (*Moshe*) to ask Pharaoh to allow the children of Israel to leave Egypt and go to the Promised Land. Instead, G-d only instructed Moses (*Moshe*) to ask Pharaoh to allow the children of Israel to take a three-day journey into the wilderness to make a sacrifice to G-d (Exodus [*Shemot*] 3:18). Moses (*Moshe*) obeyed G-d's instructions exactly as can be seen in Exodus (*Shemot*) 5:1-3. Pharaoh's first deviance of the Almighty One of Israel was his refusal to allow the people of G-d to observe a feast and to sacrifice to Him!

After a remarkable series of plagues inflicted on Egypt (*Mitzrayim*) because of Pharaoh's continued stubbornness, the children of Israel were finally released to leave Egypt laden with the spoils of the Egyptians. The children of Israel came to the banks of the Red Sea on the seventeenth day of Aviv/Nisan, which is three days after the day of Passover in the first month of the religious calendar. The Passover Lamb was slain on the fourteenth of Nisan and the people left Egypt (*Mitzrayim*) before midnight in the evening of the fifteenth after the L-rd struck the firstborn of Egypt (*Mitzrayim*). When Pharaoh saw that the children of Israel were trapped against the sea, he foolishly decided to pursue them with his army (Exodus [*Shemot*] 14:1-9). The children of Israel became afraid, but Moses (*Moshe*) rose up and said, as it is written, "...Fear ye not, stand still, and see the salvation [*Yeshooah* in Hebrew], of the Lord..." (Exodus [*Shemot*] 14:13). Jesus (*Yeshua*) in Hebrew means salvation or Savior (Matthew [*Mattityahu*] 1:21).

At this point, the sea divided and the children of Israel crossed the floor of the Red Sea on dry ground while the Egyptian army, along with Pharaoh, pursued the Hebrews into the Red Sea and were drowned (Exodus [*Shemot*] 14:26-28; 15:4,19). The Bible says that the L-rd's right hand destroyed the Egyptians (Exodus [*Shemot*] 15:6,12). The right hand is a term for the Messiah, *Yeshua* (Psalms [*Tehillim*] 44:3; 48:10; 63:8; 74:10-11; 89:13; 98:1; 110:1; 118:16; 138:7; Isaiah [*Yeshayahu*] 41:10; 53:1-5; 62:8; Acts 2:32-36; 5:31-32; Hebrews 1:3).

It is important to note that Pharaoh, along with his army, drowned in the sea. In the days of Joseph (*Yosef*), there was a famine in Israel and the children of Israel went down to Egypt (*Mitzrayim*) and gave themselves to rulership under Pharaoh. Because of this, Pharaoh had legal ownership over the people. This ownership could be broken only by the death of Pharaoh, thus freeing the children of Israel to go to the Promised Land. Because of this fact, G-d did not violate His word to Pharaoh through Moses (*Moshe*) when he asked Pharaoh to let the people go on a three-day journey into the wilderness, but later continued to go to the Promised Land. When Pharaoh died, his rulership over the children of Israel was legally broken and the people were free to go to the Promised Land. For this reason, the season of Passover (*Pesach*) is called "The Feast of Our Freedom."

Spiritually speaking, Pharaoh is a type of satan (*Ha satan*). Until you accept the Messiah (*Yeshua*) into your life, satan (*Ha satan*) has legal ownership over you. By the death of *Yeshua* (Jesus), the legal ownership that satan (*Ha satan*) has over our lives is broken and we are free to enter into the spiritual promised land of G-d and receive all the promises that He has promised us.

Fifty Days From the Red Sea: *Shavuot* (Pentecost)

From the crossing of the Red Sea (Nisan 17) to the day Moses (*Moshe*) met G-d on Mount Sinai were 47 days. For 47 days the children of Israel traveled through the wilderness before they came to Mount Sinai on the third day of the third month (Sivan) (Exodus [*Shemot*] 19:1). G-d instructed the people through Moses (*Moshe*) to sanctify themselves before He visited them three days later on Mount Sinai, which would be the sixth day of the third month of Sivan (Exodus [*Shemot*] 19:10-11). This day would be the fiftieth day following the crossing of the Red Sea; it came to be known as the revelation of G-d at Mount Sinai. This day being the fiftieth day from the crossing of the Red Sea on Nisan 17 would be the Feast of Weeks (*Shavuot*), or Pentecost.

Therefore, from the Exodus story, we can see that the Lamb was slain on the fourteenth of Nisan, the day of Passover (*Pesach*). On the fifteenth of Nisan, the day of Unleavened Bread (*Hag HaMatzah*), the people left Egypt; on the seventeenth of Nisan the children of Israel crossed the Red Sea; and 50 days later on the Feast of Weeks (*Shavuot*), or Pentecost, G-d gave the Torah (instruction) on Mount Sinai. In the following chapters, we will see how *Yeshua* (Jesus) died on Passover (*Pesach*) (Nisan 14), was in the sepulcher on the day of Unleavened Bread (*Hag HaMatzah*) (Nisan 15), and was resurrected on the day of First Fruits (*Bikkurim*) (Nisan 17), and the Holy Spirit empowered the believers 50 days following *Yeshua's* (Jesus) resurrection on the day of Pentecost (*Shavuot*). We will also discover what these feasts mean to the individual believer and how they relate to our personal relationship with G-d.

Fall Festival Overview

The fall festival season begins with a 40-day period called, in Hebrew, *Teshuvah*, which means "to repent or return." This 40-day period begins in the sixth month of the religious calendar, the month of Elul, and concludes on the tenth day of the seventh month, which is *Yom Kippur*, the day of Atonement. Each morning in the synagogue following the morning prayers, a shofar is blown (except on sabbaths and the day preceding *Rosh HaShanah*, the Feast of Trumpets). Psalm (*Tehillim*) 27 is read every day. *Rosh HaShanah* is the thirtieth day into this 40-day period of *Teshuvah* or repentance. The biblical name for *Rosh HaShanah* is *Yom Teruah*, which means "the day of the awakening blast." Non-Jews call this the Feast of Trumpets. It is observed on the seventh month (Tishrei) and the first day of the month (Leviticus [*Vayikra*] 23:23-24). G-d gave us this day to teach us about the resurrection of the dead, the coronation of the Messiah, the wedding of the Messiah, and much more. This day is both the Jewish New Year and the beginning of a period of soul-searching known as the High Holy Days, culminating on *Yom Kippur*. Therefore, the last 10 days of the 40-day period of *Teshuvah*, beginning on Elul 1, is also called the High Holy Days.

The first and second days of the 10 High Holy Days (Tishrei 1-10) are collectively known as one day (Nehemiah 7:73; 8:1-2,13). The seven-day period from Tishrei 3 through Tishrei 9 is called the Days of Awe or the Awesome Days (*Yamim Nora'im*). G-d gave these special days on His calendar to teach us about the future tribulation period on earth (*Chevlai shel Mashiach*). These seven days will correspond to the seven years of the tribulation known in Hebrew as the "birthpangs of the Messiah" (*Chevlai shel Mashiach*).

Yom Kippur (the Day of Atonement) is observed on the tenth day of the seventh month (Leviticus [*Vayikra*] 23:26-32). Since *Rosh HaShanah* teaches us about the resurrection of the dead, the coronation of the Messiah and the wedding of the Messiah, and the Days of Awe teach us about the tribulation (*Chevlai shel Mashiach*), *Yom Kippur* teaches us about the literal second coming of the Messiah *Yeshua* when He will set His foot down on the Mount of Olives (Zechariah 14:4).

The Feast of Tabernacles (*Sukkot*) is observed the fifteenth day of the seventh month of Tishrei to the twenty-first day. This festival teaches us the joy of the Messianic Kingdom, known in Hebrew as the *Athid Lavo* or to non-Jews as the Millennium. This can be found in Leviticus (*Vayikra*) 23:33-44. The day following the twenty-first day of Tishrei, the last day of *Sukkot*, is a special day called *Shemini Atzeret*.

It is known as the eighth day (Leviticus [*Vayikra*] 23:36) and is the twenty-second day of Tishrei.

Another festival called *Simchat Torah* is observed in conjunction with *Shemini Atzeret*. *Simchat* means "rejoicing" in Hebrew, so *Simchat Torah* means "rejoicing in the Torah." In ancient times, this festival was observed on the twenty-second of Tishrei, the same day as *Shemini Atzeret*. Today it is celebrated on the twenty-third of Tishrei. The celebration of *Shemini Atzeret* and *Simchat Torah* spans a 48-hour period, but it is referred to as "one long day." It is only one of two instances in the biblical year when there is a 48-hour period known as one long day. The other is *Rosh HaShanah*, which spans the first and second days of Tishrei. *Shemini Atzeret* and *Simchat Torah* were given by G-d to teach us how things will be following the Messianic age or the Millennium when the world will enter into eternity.

Feasts of the L-rd

Biblical/Hebrew Name	English Name	Time of Observance
1. Pesach	Passover	Nisan/Aviv 14
2. Hag HaMatzah	Feast of Unleavened Bread	Nisan/Aviv 15-21
3. Bikkurim	First Fruits of Barley Harvest	The morrow after the sabbath during Hag HaMatzah
4. Shavuot	Feast of Weeks/Pentecost	Fifty days from the Feast of First Fruits
5. Yom Teruah (Rosh HaShanah)	Feast of Trumpets	Tishrei 1
6. Yom Kippur	Day of Atonement	Tishrei 10
7. Sukkot	Feast of Tabernacles/Booths	Tishrei 15-21
a. Shemini Atzeret	The eighth assembly/conclusion	Tishrei 22
b. Simchat Torah	Rejoicing in the Torah	Tishrei 23

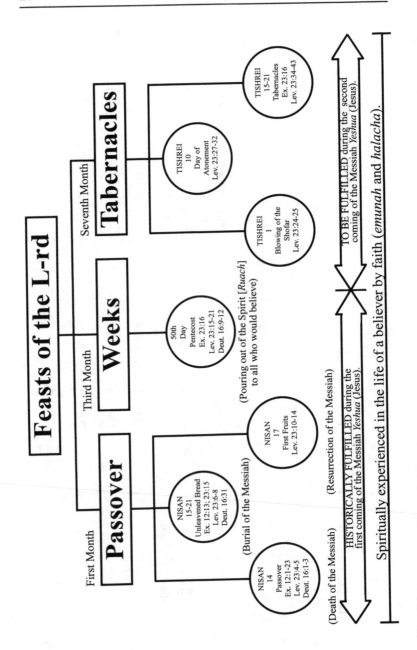

Feasts of the L-rd

Passover

First Month

NISAN 14
Passover
Ex. 12:1-23
Lev. 23:4-5
Deut. 16:1-3

(Death of the Messiah)

NISAN 15-21
Unleavened Bread
Ex. 12:13; 23:15
Lev. 23:6-8
Deut. 16:31

(Burial of the Messiah)

NISAN 17
First Fruits
Lev. 23:10-14

(Resurrection of the Messiah)

Weeks

Third Month

50th Day
Pentecost
Ex. 23:16
Lev. 23:15-21
Deut. 16:9-12

(Pouring out of the Spirit [*Ruach*] to all who would believe)

Tabernacles

Seventh Month

TISHREI 1
Blowing of the Shofar
Lev. 23:24-25

TISHREI 10
Day of Atonement
Lev. 23:27-32

TISHREI 15-21
Tabernacles
Ex. 23:16
Lev. 23:34-43

HISTORICALLY FULFILLED during the first coming of the Messiah *Yeshua* (Jesus).

TO BE FULFILLED during the second coming of the Messiah *Yeshua* (Jesus).

Spiritually experienced in the life of a believer by faith (*emunah* and *halacha*).

Feasts of the L-rd

Feast	Historical Aspect	Messianic Fulfillment	Spiritual Application (*Halacha*)
Passover (Pesach)	Israel's deliverance out of Egyptian bondage	Death of *Yeshua* on the tree	Repent (*teshuvah*) and trust by faith (*emunah*) in the shed blood of *Yeshua*
Unleavened Bread (Hag HaMatzah)	The going out of Egypt	Burial of *Yeshua*	Sanctification and separation from evil represented by water immersion (*mikvah*)
First Fruits (Bikkurim)	Crossing the Red Sea	Resurrection of *Yeshua*	Walking (*halacha*) in newness of life
Pentecost (Shavuot)	Giving of the Torah at Mount Sinai	Pouring out of the Holy Spirit (*Ruach HaKodesh*) on Shavuot	Immersion in the Holy Spirit (*Ruach HaKodesh*) and growing in faith (*emunah*) in G-d (making spiritual *aliyah*)
Rosh HaShanah (Yom Teruah)	Blowing the shofar Jewish New Year	The resurrection of the dead/rapture (*Natzal*) of believers	Hear (*shema*) the calling (*shofar*) of G-d for our lives
Day of Atonement (Yom Kippur)	Priest entered the Holy of Holies Cleansing of people's sins	The day of the Messiah's second coming	Yielding ourselves to G-d so we may live (face to face) in His presence
Tabernacles (Sukkot)	Entering the Promised Land/Great rejoicing	The Messianic era/Millennium (*Athid Lavo*)	A daily rest (*shabbat*) in the Messiah and having the rest (*menuchah*) of His Kingdom be in our hearts

Chapter 3

Passover (*Pesach*): Feasting for Freedom

And ye shall observe this thing [Passover] *for an ordinance to thee and to thy sons for ever. ...And it shall come to pass, when your children shall say unto you, What mean ye by this service? that ye shall say, It is the sacrifice of the Lord's passover, who passed over the houses of the children of Israel in Egypt...*(Exodus [*Shemot*] 12:24,26-27).

Understanding the Passover (*Pesach*) Season

G-d declared Passover (*Pesach*) to be a permanent celebration for all eternity (Exodus [*Shemot*] 12:2,6,13-14). Historically, Passover (*Pesach*) celebrates G-d's deliverance of the children of Israel from bondage in Egypt (*Mitzrayim*), where they were slaves to the Egyptians (Exodus [*Shemot*] 2:23-24; 6:5-8; 13:3,14).

The spiritual application that G-d wants us to understand is this: Egypt (*Mitzrayim*) is a type of the world and the world's system. Its ruler, Pharaoh, was a type of satan (*Ha satan*). The bondage people are in when they live according to the ways of the world's system is sin (John [*Yochanan*] 8:34).

Historically, the children of Israel were delivered from the bondage in Egypt (*Mitzrayim*) by putting the blood of a lamb upon the doorposts of their houses (Exodus [*Shemot*] 12:2,6,13). Spiritually, this is a picture of the Messiah *Yeshua* and how those who believe in Him are delivered from the bondages of sin and the rule of satan (*Ha satan*) in their lives. *Yeshua* is the Lamb of G-d (John [*Yochanan*] 1:29). *Yeshua* is also our Passover (*Pesach*) (1 Corinthians 5:7). Those who follow *Yeshua* are the house of G-d (Hebrews 3:6; 1 Peter [*Kefa*] 2:5). The doorposts are our hearts. It is only through trusting by faith (*emunah*) in the shed blood of *Yeshua* (Jesus), our Passover (*Pesach*), that we are free from the bondage of sin (Galatians 4:3-5,9; 5:1; 2 Peter [*Kefa*] 2:19). This is because the blood of *Yeshua* redeems us from sin (Leviticus [*Vayikra*] 17:11; Ephesians 1:7; Colossians 1:14; 1 Peter [*Kefa*] 1:18-19; 1 John [*Yochanan*] 1:7; Revelation 1:5).

During Passover (*Pesach*), the head of each household was to take a lamb of the first year on the tenth day of the first month known as Nisan and set it aside until the fourteenth day (Exodus [*Shemot*] 12:3-6). In the evening of the fourteenth day, at exactly 3:00 p.m., the lamb was to be killed (Exodus [*Shemot*] 12:6). The blood of the lamb was to be sprinkled on the lintel and two side posts of the household door. The lamb was to be roasted with fire, with bitter herbs, and with unleavened bread, and the entire household was to feast upon the body of the lamb (Exodus [*Shemot*] 12:7-8). The people were instructed by G-d to eat the lamb with haste and to be dressed and ready to leave Egypt (*Mitzrayim*) at the midnight hour. This would be the fifteenth day of Nisan (Exodus [*Shemot*] 12:10-11).

At midnight on that fateful evening in Egypt, death passed through the land. Every house that did not have the token of the blood on the doorposts and lintel suffered the judgment of G-d (Exodus [*Shemot*] 12:12-15). The Hebrew word for Passover is *Pesach*, which means "to pass or hover over." This word speaks to us about two things. First, it shows the passing over in judgment from death and sin to life in *Yeshua*. Second, it tells us about allowing, by faith (*emunah*), the blood of *Yeshua* to hover over our lives and give us divine protection from the evil one (*Ha satan*).

God's Commandments (*Mitzvot*) for Passover (*Pesach*)

1. **Passover was the beginning of months** (Exodus [*Shemot*] 12:2).

    *Spiritual Application (**Halacha**).* Nisan is the first month of the religious calendar. Receiving *Yeshua* into our lives is the beginning of a New Covenant (*Brit Hadashah*) relationship with G-d (Jeremiah [*Yermiyahu*] 31:31-33; John [*Yochanan*] 3:5-7; Romans 6:1-4; 2 Corinthians 5:17). Passover is the first of the feasts. Likewise, repenting of our sins (*teshuvah*) and believing in the shed blood of *Yeshua* is our first step in our walk (*halacha*) with G-d.

2. **The lamb was hidden for four days** (Exodus [*Shemot*] 12:3,6).

    Messianic Fulfillment. G-d commanded Israel to take a lamb on the tenth day of Nisan and set it aside until the fourteenth day. These four days were fulfilled by *Yeshua* during the Passover (*Pesach*) week. Remember, *Yeshua* is the Lamb of G-d (John [*Yochanan*] 1:29). He entered Jerusalem (*Yerushalayim*) and went to the temple (*Beit HaMikdash*), which was the house of G-d, and went on public display there for four days from Nisan 10 to Nisan 14 (Matthew [*Mattityahu*] 21:1,9-12,17-18,23; 24:1,3; 26:1-5).

Eschatologically, these four days that the lamb was hidden is prophetic of the people's expectations that the Messiah would come 4,000 years from the creation of Adam as part of the 7,000-year plan of G-d to redeem both man and the earth back to how things were in the Garden of Eden (*Gan Eden*) (Mishnah, San Hedrin 97-98). These four days are prophetic of the Messiah *Yeshua* being hid from the world and not coming to earth for four days or 4,000 years from the creation of Adam. A day is understood to be prophetic of a thousand years, based upon Psalm (*Tehillim*) 90:4 and Second Peter (*Kefa*) 3:8. Linking Psalm 90:4 to each day in creation, G-d ordained each day in creation to be prophetic of a thousand years of time and the entire redemption to take 7,000 years to complete from the fall of man in the Garden of Eden (Genesis [*Bereishit*] 1:1,5,8,13,19,23,31; 2:1-3).

3. **The lamb was to be without blemish** (Exodus [*Shemot*] 12:5).

Messianic Fulfillment. *Yeshua* was the Lamb of G-d (John [*Yochanan*] 1:29) without spot or blemish (1 Peter [*Kefa*] 1:18-20). During the crucifixion week, *Yeshua* was examined by many in fulfilling this Scripture, including: (a) the chief priests and elders (Matthew [*Mattityahu*] 21:23);

(b) Pilate (Matthew [*Mattityahu*] 27:1-2,11-14,17-26); (c) Herod (Luke 23:6-12); (d) Annas the high priest (*Cohen Ha-Gadol*) (Luke 3:2; John [*Yochanan*] 18:13,24); (e) Caiaphas the high priest (John [*Yochanan*] 11:49-53; 18:13-14,19-24, 28); (f) Judas (Matthew [*Mattityahu*] 27:3-10); (g) the centurion (Matthew [*Mattityahu*] 27:54); (h) the repentant thief (Luke 23:39-43).

When we examine *Yeshua*, we must conclude also that He was without blot or blemish.

4.   The lamb was of the first year (Exodus [*Shemot*] 11:4-7; 12:5).

Spiritual Application (*Halacha*). G-d always distinguishes between the believers and the world (Exodus [*Shemot*] 12:29-30). This can be seen in the examples that follow. The firstborn of both man and beast was to be set aside and given to G-d (Exodus [*Shemot*] 13:2,11-13). The theme of the firstborn runs throughout the Bible. Cain was set aside for Abel (Genesis [*Bereishit*] 4:1-8); Ishmael for Isaac (*Yitzchak*) (Genesis [*Bereishit*] 16:1,11-12,15; 17:17-19); Esau for Jacob (*Ya'akov*) (Genesis [*Bereishit*] 25:19-26; Romans 9:8-13); and Egypt (*Mitzrayim*) for Israel.

Spiritually, G-d gave us these examples to teach us that the firstborn after the flesh (that which is natural) is set aside to bring forth the firstborn after the spirit (that which is spiritual). In this process, G-d distinguishes between the first or natural birth and the second or spiritual birth. The first birth constitutes us as sinners and the second birth makes us believers and children of G-d (John [*Yochanan*] 1:12; 3:1-7; Romans 9:8-13; 1 Corinthians 15:22; 15:45-47).

Messianic Fulfillment. Yeshua was the firstborn of Mary (*Miryam*) naturally, and the firstborn of G-d spiritually (Matthew [*Mattityahu*] 1:21-25; Romans 8:29; Colossians 1:15,18; Revelation 3:14).

5.   **It is a male** (Exodus [*Shemot*] 12:5).

Spiritual Application (Halacha). It was through one man's sin that sin came into the world (Romans 5:12; 1 Timothy 2:12-14). Because Adam, the first male, sinned, so a male, *Yeshua*, must die to atone for that sin (Romans 5:17-19).

6.   **It is a lamb for a house** (Exodus [*Shemot*] 12:3-4).

Spiritual Application (Halacha). G-d's intention was that all (households) experience salvation. The lamb was a lamb for the house. By believing in the Messiah *Yeshua*, we become members of the household of faith (Galatians 6:10; Ephesians 2:19). Salvation for a household is available to all who believe in the Messiah, *Yeshua*, the Lamb of G-d (Genesis [*Bereishit*] 7:1; 18:16-19; Joshua [*Yehoshua*] 24:15; John [*Yochanan*] 4:46-54; Luke 19:5-10; Acts 16:15,31; 18:3,8).

Messianic Fulfillment. There is a progressive revelation of the Lamb in the Bible. First, there is a lamb for a house (Exodus [*Shemot*] 12:3-4); second, a lamb for a nation (John [*Yochanan*] 11:49-52); and finally, a lamb for the world (John [*Yochanan*] 1:29).

Genesis (*Bereishit*) 22 is known in Hebrew as the *Akeidah*, or the binding of the sacrifice. In Genesis (*Bereishit*) 22:7, Isaac (*Yitzchak*) asked, "Where is the lamb?" The lamb that Isaac (*Yitzchak*) asked about is *Yeshua* (Isaiah [*Yeshayahu*] 53:7).

7.   A Passover (*Pesach*) lamb was to be killed between the evenings (Exodus [*Shemot*] 12:6).

The biblical day goes from evening to evening, from sundown to sundown, which is roughly 6:00 p.m. to 6:00 p.m. (Genesis [*Bereishit*] 1:5,8,13,19,23,31). The day (6:00 p.m. to 6:00 p.m.) is divided into two 12-hour periods. The evening runs from 6:00 p.m. to 6:00 a.m. The morning runs from 6:00 a.m. to 6:00 p.m. Each 12-hour period is divided into two smaller portions. From 6:00 a.m. to noon is the morning part of the day. From noon to 6:00 p.m. is the evening part of the day. The phrase, "between the evening" (from Exodus [*Shemot*] 12:6) refers to the period of the day that goes from noon to 6:00 p.m., which is exactly 3:00 p.m. This would be the ninth hour of the day, counting from 6:00 a.m.

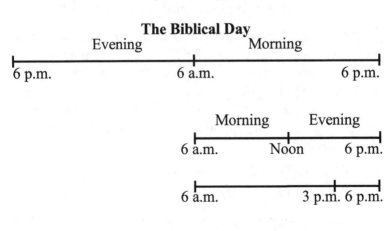

The Biblical Day

Evening   Morning

6 p.m.   6 a.m.   6 p.m.

Morning   Evening

6 a.m.   Noon   6 p.m.

6 a.m.   3 p.m. 6 p.m.

The 9th hour of the day = 3 p.m.

Messianic Fulfillment. *Yeshua* died at the ninth hour of the day (Matthew [*Mattityahu*] 27:45-50). This would be exactly 3:00 p.m. (the ninth hour, counting from 6:00 a.m.).

8. The whole assembly shall kill it (Exodus [*Shemot*] 12:6).

Spiritual Application (Halacha). Every person who has ever lived on planet Earth and sinned is guilty of killing *Yeshua* because He died for all sinners (Romans 3:10,23). No human being had the power to take His life (John [*Yochanan*] 10:17-18). Therefore, *Yeshua* laid down His life for us by His own free will. There has been a misplaced accusation over the years that the Jews were the people who killed *Yeshua*. As a result, they have suffered horrendously over the centuries. To my beloved Jewish friends who are reading this book, I ask you with sincere repentance (*teshuvah*): Please forgive those who are ignorant of the truth. The truth is that **I** killed *Yeshua*, as did everyone who ever lived on planet Earth, because He died for *my* sins! (Romans 5:8,12)

Messianic Fulfillment. A whole congregation of people was involved in the death of *Yeshua*. The Gospels of Matthew (*Mattityahu*), Mark, Luke, and John (*Yochanan*) show how the Sanhedrin, the priests, the Romans, and the people of Israel all clamored for the crucifixion of *Yeshua* and for His blood to be shed (Matthew [*Mattityahu*] 27:17,20-22,25; Acts 4:26-28).

9. The blood must be applied to the door (Exodus [*Shemot*] 12:7,13,22).

Spiritual Application (Halacha). Those who believe in the Messiah are the house of G-d (Ephesians 2:19; 1 Timothy 3:15; Hebrews 3:6). The only way into the house of G-d is through the shed blood of the Messiah *Yeshua*, who is the Door (John [*Yochanan*] 10:7-9).

10. The body of the lamb must be eaten (Exodus [*Shemot*] 12:8-10).

Spiritual Application (*Halacha*). Both the body and blood of the lamb speak of the body and blood of *Yeshua* (Matthew [*Mattityahu*] 26:26-28). We spiritually eat of the body of the Lamb (*Yeshua*) when we eat of His body (today represented by the bread), which spiritually is the Word of G-d (Luke 11:3; 4:4). By following the Word of G-d and obeying the commandments (*mitzvot*) of G-d with sincerity of heart, we eat (spiritually) of His body.

a. It must be eaten the same night (Exodus [*Shemot*] 12:8). *Yeshua* was crucified, suffered, and died the same night.

b. It must be eaten with unleavened bread (Exodus [*Shemot*] 12:8). Leaven speaks of sin (1 Corinthians 5:6-8). Unleavened bread is without sin. As believers, we are instructed to live holy (unleavened) lives before G-d (Leviticus [*Vayikra*] 11:44; 19:2; 1 Peter [*Kefa*] 1:15-16).

c. It must be eaten with bitter herbs (Exodus [*Shemot*] 12:8).

    Spiritual Application (*Halacha*). To those who have accepted the Messiah into their lives, bitter herbs speak of two things. First, they speak of the bondage and burdens we experience while living in this world (a type of Egypt) before we accepted *Yeshua* into our lives. This burden of sin is placed on us by satan (*Ha satan*) when we yield to his lies and deception, and then sin because of our own evil desires. Second, the bitter herbs speak of the bitter things that come into our lives after we accept *Yeshua* and attempt to follow Him on a daily basis.

Messianic Fulfillment. For *Yeshua*, dying on the tree was a bitter experience because He had to pay for man's sin with His sinless life.

d. The lamb must be roasted in fire (Exodus [*Shemot*] 12:8).

Spiritual Application (*Halacha*). Fire speaks of judgment, refining, and purification. Our faith (*emunah*) is judged and tested by fire so it can be refined and purified and come forth as pure gold (Zechariah 13:9; James [*Ya'akov*] 1:12; 1 Peter [*Kefa*] 1:7; Revelation 3:18).

e. It must not be sodden with water. The gospel (*basar*) of *Yeshua* must not be watered down (Mark 7:9,13; 2 Timothy 3:5).

f. The head, legs, and other parts of the lamb must be eaten.

Spiritual Application (*Halacha*). Those who believe in *Yeshua* must feed on the mind of *Yeshua* (Philippians 2:5; 1 Corinthians 2:16; Romans 12:2; Ephesians 4:21-23; Hebrews 8:10). The legs speak of our walk (*halacha*) (Colossians 2:6). How are the believers in *Yeshua* to walk? (See Romans 6:4; 8:1,4; 2 Corinthians 5:7; Galatians 5:16; Ephesians 2:10;

5:2,8; Colossians 1:10, 4:5; 1 Thessalonians 4:1;
1 John [*Yochanan*] 1:7; 2 John 1:6; 3 John 1:4.)

11. The lamb must be eaten in haste (Exodus [*Shemot*]
12:11).

Spiritual Application (*Halacha*). Bible believers must be
quick to leave Egypt (the influences of the world) and run toward the life that is in the Messiah (Luke 19:5-6).

a. It must be eaten with our loins girded (Exodus
[*Shemot*] 12:11). Our loins being girded speaks
about our hearts' desire to eagerly serve and obey
G-d. Our spiritual loins are the truth of the Word of
G-d (Ephesians 6:14). Scriptures that speak about
our loins being girded include the following: First
Kings (*Melachim*) 18:46; Second Kings (*Melachim*)
4:29; 9:1; Jeremiah (*Yermiyahu*) 1:17; Luke 12:35;
Ephesians 6:14; First Peter (*Kefa*) 1:13.

b. Shoes must be on our feet (Exodus [Shemot] 12:11).
Shoes on our feet speaks about our walk with God.
Scriptures that speak about shoes being on our feet in-
clude the following: Isaiah [Yeshayahu] 52:7; Nahum
[Nachum] 1:15; Romans 10:15; Ephesians 6:15.

c. A staff must be in our hand (Exodus [*Shemot*]
12:11). A staff in our hand speaks about the believer's authority in the Kingdom of G-d by the
name of *Yeshua* (Matthew [*Mattityahu*] 28:18-20).
Scriptures that speak about a staff being in our hand
include the following: Genesis (*Bereishit*) 38:17-18;
Exodus (*Shemot*) 14:16; Judges (*Shoftim*) 6:21; First
Samuel (*Sh'muwel*) 17:39-40; Second Samuel

(*Sh'muwel*) 3:29; Second Kings (*Melachim*) 4:29; 18:21; Psalm (*Tehillim*) 23:4; Isaiah (*Yeshayahu*) 10:24; 14:5; Mark 6:7-8.

12. It is the L-rd's Passover (Exodus [*Shemot*] 12:11).

***Spiritual Application* (*Halacha*).** If we follow *Yeshua* with all of our hearts, we will pass from death to life, and from judgment to divine protection (John [*Yochanan*] 5:24; 1 John [*Yochanan*] 3:14; 2 Corinthians 5:17; Psalm [*Tehillim*] 91).

13. It is a memorial (Exodus [*Shemot*] 12:14; Luke 22:1,7-8, 13-15,19).

***Spiritual Application* (*Halacha*).** Passover (*Pesach*) is a memorial or a remembrance (Luke 22:1,7-8,13-15,19). There are two elements of remembrance:

a. **G-d remembers us** (Genesis [*Bereishit*] 8:1; 9:1, 5-16; 19:29; 30:22; Exodus [*Shemot*] 2:24-25; 3:1; 6:2,5; 32:1-3,7,11,13-14; Leviticus [*Vayikra*] 26:14,31-33,38-45; Numbers [*Bamidbar*] 10:1-2,9; Psalm [*Tehillim*] 105:7-8; 42:2-3; 112:6). In fact, G-d has a book of remembrance (Exodus [*Shemot*] 32:32-33; Malachi 3:16-18; Revelation 3:5; 20:11-15; 21:1,27).

b. **We must remember G-d** (Exodus [*Shemot*] 13:3; 20:8; Deuteronomy [*Devarim*] 7:17-19; 8:18; 16:3; Numbers [*Bamidbar*] 15:37-41).

14. It is to be observed at the going down of the sun (Deuteronomy [*Devarim*] 16:2,6). This was fulfilled by *Yeshua* at His crucifixion (Matthew [*Mattityahu*] 27:45-46).

15. **It is the place where G-d would put His name** (Deuteronomy [*Devarim*] 16:2,6).

Messianic Fulfillment. The place where G-d has put His name is Jerusalem (*Yerushalayim*) (2 Kings [*Melachim*] 21:4). *Yeshua* was crucified in Jerusalem (*Yerushalayim*).

16. **Not a bone of the lamb was to be broken** (Exodus [*Shemot*] 12:43-46).

Messianic Fulfillment. Not a bone of *Yeshua* was broken on the tree (John [*Yochanan*] 19:33).

17. **There was to be an explanation of the service** (Exodus [*Shemot*] 12:25-28).

Messianic Fulfillment. *Yeshua* explained each part of the Passover (*Pesach*) as He did the service (Luke 22:14-20; 1 Corinthians 11:23-26).

18. **The Egyptians were spoiled at the Exodus** (Exodus [*Shemot*] 12:31-36).

Messianic Fulfillment. Satan was spoiled when *Yeshua* entered hell and rose again (Colossians 2:15).

19. **You must be circumcised to eat the Passover** (Exodus [*Shemot*] 12:48; Joshua [*Yehoshua*] 5:2-10).

Spiritual Application (Halacha). The physical act of circumcision was only a picture of the inward or spiritual circumcision that G-d wanted us to have (Romans 2:28-29; 1 Corinthians 15:46; 2 Corinthians 4:18). God has always desired for His people to be circumcised in the heart (Deuteronomy

[*Devarim*] 10:12-16; 1 Corinthians 7:18-19; Galatians 2:3; 5:2-3; 6:12-15; Ephesians 2:11-13).

20. The Passover (*Pesach*) feast was to be a holy convo-cation, and no work was to be done (Exodus [*Shemot*] 12:16).

Spiritual Application (Halacha). A believer finds true rest in ceasing from his own works and resting in the finished work of *Yeshua*, G-d's Passover (*Pesach*) Lamb (Genesis [*Bereishit*] 2:1-2; Matthew [*Mattityahu*] 11:28-30; John [*Yochanan*] 17:1-4; 19:30; Hebrews 3:14-19; 4:1-10).

21. The Passover (*Pesach*) must be killed outside the gates of the city (Deuteronomy [*Devarim*] 16:5).

Messianic Fulfillment. *Yeshua* was crucified outside of the city walls of Jerusalem (*Yerushalayim*) at a place called Golgotha (John [*Yochanan*] 19:16-19; Hebrews 13:10-13).

22. There is healing power in the lamb (Exodus [*Shemot*] 15:26).

Messianic Fulfillment. *Yeshua* is the Healer sent from G-d (Psalm [*Tehillim*] 105:36-38; Isaiah [*Yeshayahu*] 53:1-5; 1 Peter [*Kefa*] 2:24; 1 Corinthians 11:26-30).

23. The Exodus was on eagle's wings (Exodus [*Shemot*] 19:4).

Scriptures associated with this are Deuteronomy (*Devarim*) 32:9-13; Isaiah (*Yeshayahu*) 31:5; 40:31; Luke 17:33-37; Revelation 12:6,14.

24. They sang a song of rejoicing to the L-rd (Exodus [*Shemot*] 15:1,19-21).

***Spiritual Application* (*Halacha*).** Whenever a believer experiences and understands the meaning of Passover (*Pesach*), there is a spirit of rejoicing to the L-rd for his or her deliverance from sin, and for experiencing the newness of life in the Messiah. Note: The Passover Seder, which is the service and meal that celebrates the Passover, always ends with songs of rejoicing and the declaration: *Next year in Jerusalem!* This can be seen in Mark 14:26.

25. Israel is the firstborn of G-d (Exodus [*Shemot*] 4:22-23).

***Spiritual Application* (*Halacha*).** All those who accept the Messiah *Yeshua* are called the firstborn of G-d even as *Yeshua* is called the firstborn of G-d (Romans 8:29; Colossians 1:15,18; Hebrews 12:22-24).[1]

Did *Yeshua* Have a Passover Meal?

Today there are 15 steps in the Passover Seder. In order to understand if *Yeshua* had a Passover Seder, we need to know what is done during a Passover Seder. Therefore, I will list the 15 steps to the Passover Seder and explain what is done in each part. By doing this, we can determine if *Yeshua* had a Passover Seder prior to His crucifixion.

Before I begin to explain the 15 steps to the Passover Seder, I would like to comment on one aspect of it. During the Seder, a cup of wine is brought forth with this blessing: "Blessed are You, L-rd our G-d, King of the Universe, who creates the fruit of the vine." During the Feast of Passover (*Pesach*), *Yeshua* said, "I am the true vine" (John [*Yochanan*] 15:1). Isaiah (*Yeshayahu*) tells us that G-d had a vineyard and that vineyard was Israel (Isaiah [*Yeshayahu*] 5:7). The choice vine planted in the vineyard was the Messiah (Isaiah [*Yeshayahu*] 5:2).

The Seder Service

1. *Kaddesh* **and the first cup.**
    During the Kaddesh, the first of four cups of wine is blessed and drunk. This first cup of wine is called the cup of sanctification. Before the wine is drunk, a blessing is recited: "Blessed are You, L-rd our G-d, King of the Universe, who creates the fruit of the vine."

2. *U-r'chatz* **(the washing of hands).**
    No blessing is recited.

3. *Karpas* **(this word means "parsley, green herbs").**
    This refers to the place in the Seder when the celebrants dip a green vegetable in salt water and eat it (John [*Yochanan*] 13:26-27). The oldest will sit on the left side of the table and will dip the sop. From this, we can conclude that Judas was the oldest disciple. The youngest will sit on the right side of the table. Benjamin (*Benyamin*) was the youngest of Jacob's (*Ya'akov's*) sons. Benjamin means "son of my right hand" in Hebrew.

4. *Yachatz* **(the breaking of the bread).**
    The middle piece of three pieces of bread, or *matzot*, is ceremonially broken in two. *Matzah* (plural is *matzot*) is unleavened bread. The larger piece is wrapped in a napkin and set aside as the *afikomen*, the *matzah* that is eaten at the end of the meal. This can be seen in Luke 22:19.

5. **The *Maggid* (the telling of the story of the Exodus).**
   The *Maggid* concludes with the second cup of wine, which is called the cup of wrath. *Yeshua* partook of this second cup at the Garden of Gethsemane (Luke 22:42-44). In telling the story of the Exodus, each person is to see the Exodus as if G-d personally redeemed them! This is based upon Exodus (*Shemot*) 13:8.

6. ***Rachtzah* (the washing of hands with a blessing).**

7. ***Motzi* (the blessing over bread).**
   The blessing over the bread is as follows: "Blessed are You, L-rd our G-d, King of the Universe, who brings forth the bread from the earth." This blessing is a prophecy of the resurrection of the Messiah from the earth because He is the believer's bread (John [*Yochanan*] 6:47-51). G-d brought forth the bread (*Yeshua*) from the earth following His death (Acts 2:31-33).

8. ***Matzah* (the *Matzah* is blessed and eaten).**
   In John (*Yochanan*) 13:23, we can see that the disciples were leaning or reclining. Passover (*Pesach*) is called the season of our freedom. On this day, you are freed from the slavery of Egypt (*Mitzrayim*), symbolizing the bondage of sin, and you are seen as a king. Kings traditionally recline at their meals, and so celebrants reclined during portions of the Passover Seder. The believers in *Yeshua* are kings and priests before G-d (Revelation 1:6; 5:10).

9. ***Maror* (bitter herbs are blessed and eaten).** *Maror* is bitter herbs. These bitter herbs are symbolized by romaine lettuce and horseradish.

10. *Korech* (the *matzah* and *maror* are eaten together).

11. *Shulchan Orech* (the meal is eaten).

12. *Tzafun* (the *afikomen* that was hidden is found, ransomed, and then eaten).

13. *Barech* (grace after meals).

    At the conclusion of *Barech*, the blessing for wine is recited over the third cup. Then the cup is drunk. This is the cup of redemption (Luke 22:20; 1 Corinthians 10:16).

14. *Hallel.*

    Psalms (*Tehillim*) 115–118 are chanted in special praise to G-d. The fourth cup is now filled, and a door is opened for Elijah (*Eliyahu*) to enter and proclaim the coming of Messiah.

15. *Nirtzah* (all is finished).

    A final song is sung and ends with the phrase, *Next Year in Jerusalem!* This can be seen in Matthew 26:30 and Mark 14:26.

Yeshua ate the Passover (Luke 22:15). This Scripture passage refers specifically to the Lamb. Frequently, there were two sacrifices during the Feast of Passover. One lamb is the Passover lamb and the other lamb is called the *haggigah* or peace offering. These sacrifices are referred to in Deuteronomy (*Devarim*) 16:2 where G-d required that the sacrifice be from both the flock *and* the herd. This was interpreted to mean that two sacrifices were needed. The *Haggigah* (the additional lamb) was offered in addition to the *Pesach* (the Passover lamb). The *Pesach* was required, but the *Haggigah* was not because it was a freewill offering.

During the days of *Yeshua*, in order to have a Seder, you needed to register at a rabbinical court in the temple (*Beit HaMikdash*), and you must have at least 10 and no more than 20 people. Each group of pilgrims who came to Jerusalem (*Yerushalayim*) had one representative carrying a lamb without spot or blemish (Exodus [*Shemot*] 12:4-5). An assembly of at least 10 people (known in Hebrew as a *minyan*) was required to participate in the ceremony.

Each group of people entered the temple (*Beit HaMidkash*) with their lamb. They were instructed, "You must slay the lamb, not the priests." The priests caught the blood and ministered the blood according to the Scriptures. The only place where a Passover (*Pesach*) lamb could be killed was in Jerusalem (*Yerushalayim*). Therefore, those who couldn't come to Jerusalem (*Yerushalayim*) to keep the Passover (*Pesach*), but still wanted to keep the meal, would have to have a substitute for the Passover (*Pesach*) lamb. That substitute was the shankbone of a lamb. It has a special name in Hebrew: *zeroah*, or arm. *Yeshua* was referred to as the *zeroah* or arm of the L-rd in Isaiah (*Yeshayahu*) 53:1. The shankbone or *zeroah* will be a remembrance of the lamb that was slain.

The Passover (*Pesach*) requirement is that you must eat until you are full. The entire lamb must be consumed before midnight on the fifteenth of Nisan. If you had only 10 people, you would not want to have two lambs because they could not be totally eaten in time. This would violate the commandment (*mitzvah*) that the lamb was to be eaten before midnight (Exodus [*Shemot*] 12:8). If you had 20 people, one lamb would not be enough to make everyone full, and this would also violate the commandment (*mitzvah*) given by G-d. Therefore, if you had 20 people, you would need two lambs.

Once again, *Yeshua* ate the Passover (Luke 22:15). You can have a Seder without a *Pesach* (or Passover lamb), but you cannot have a lamb without a Seder. Also, since *Yeshua* was the Passover Lamb of G-d (John [*Yochanan*] 1:29), He had to come to Jerusalem (*Yerushalayim*) from Bethany not only to be the Passover (*Pesach*) lamb, but also for the Seder (Mark 14:3,12-16). So, *Yeshua* was having a Passover lamb (Luke 22:15), and it was a Seder. Today, there is no temple (*Beit HaMikdash*), so the Passover Seder is held on the fifteenth or sixteenth of Nisan. The Seder on the fifteenth is called the First Seder, and the Seder on the sixteenth is called the Second Seder.

In Mark 14:12, it is written, "And the first day of unleavened bread, when they killed the passover [the *Pesach* lamb]...." The word translated as first is the Greek word *protos*, which means "before, earlier, and preceding." Because there was a temple (*Beit HaMikdash*) in Jerusalem (*Yerushalayim*) in the days of *Yeshua*, the First Seder would be on the fourteenth of Nisan, and the Second Seder on the fifteenth. The Seder could be held on either night. *Yeshua* had His Passover (*Pesach*) Seder by midnight on the fourteenth of Nisan (remember that the fourteenth of Nisan begins at sundown, which is roughly six hours prior to midnight), and was crucified the next afternoon at 3:00 p.m., which is still the fourteenth of Nisan.

The high priest (*Cohen HaGadol*) kills the Passover (*Pesach*) lamb for the nation of Israel at 3:00 p.m. on the fourteenth of Nisan. At sundown, the fifteenth begins, so *Yeshua* would have to eat His Passover lamb by midnight of the fourteenth of Nisan, which is prior to the time that the high priest kills the Passover lamb for the nation. To further prove this, in John (*Yochanan*) 18:28, when *Yeshua* was brought before Pilate, Caiaphas the high priest (*Cohen HaGadol*) wouldn't enter the judgment hall of the Gentile ruler because he would be defiled and couldn't eat the Passover lamb. So, this event must have taken place on the morning of the fourteenth of Nisan because the high priest had not yet eaten the Passover. If he was defiled, he would be defiled for one day. Since *Yeshua* had already eaten the Passover by the time He was seized and taken before Caiaphas and Pilate, He had to have eaten the Passover with the disciples on the evening of the fourteenth. Thus, we can see how *Yeshua* ate a *Passover* meal and could still fulfill being the Passover Lamb of G-d by being killed at 3:00 p.m. on the fourteenth of Nisan.[2]

The Bread and Cups of the Passover Seder

During the celebration of *Pesach*, three cakes of unleavened bread (*matzot*) are placed one upon another, with a napkin between each cake. At a certain point in the Seder service, the middle cake, known as the *afikomen*, or "that which come after," is broken in two. One piece is distributed among the people present, and the larger piece is hidden in a napkin. Toward the end of the Passover Seder, the hidden portion is brought to light and eaten by those surrounding the Passover table. The Messianic understanding is that these three pieces of *matzot* represent G-d the Father, the Messiah *Yeshua*, and the Holy Spirit (*Ruach HaKodesh*). The central piece, the *afikomen*, is broken, a portion is eaten, and the remainder hidden and then brought forth to testify of the death, burial, and resurrection of *Yeshua*.

During the course of the Seder, the four cups of wine that are served to the people present at the Seder are used in the following manner, and are called:

1. **The cup of blessing** (Luke 22:17; 1 Corinthians 10:16). This cup is called the cup of sanctification, or the *Kiddush*.

2. **The cup of wrath** (Luke 22:42-44). This cup is not drunk, but is poured out on the table as the plagues of Egypt are recited. *Yeshua* drank of this cup for us in the Garden of Gethsemane and when He died on the tree.

3. **The cup of blessing, salvation, or redemption**. This cup is filled to overflowing, symbolizing an overflowing salvation (Psalm [*Tehillim*] 116:13).

4. **The cup of the kingdom** (Luke 22:18,20; Matthew [*Mattityahu*] 26:28-29). *Yeshua* spoke of eating and drinking afresh in the Messianic age with His disciples after His resurrection.

In addition to the four cups of wine served to the people, another cup, called the cup of Elijah (*Eliyahu*), is also a part of the Seder. This cup is poured out at the end of the Seder. Only Elijah (*Eliyahu*) himself, or one coming in the spirit and power of Elijah, or the Messiah, was allowed to drink of this cup. When *Yeshua* referred to Himself drinking of this cup, He was saying in no uncertain terms that He was the Messiah.

How Did *Yeshua* Fulfill the Passover?

The Feast of Passover (*Pesach*) was given by G-d to be a rehearsal (*miqra*) of the first coming of *Yeshua*. The Passover ceremony was observed in remembrance of the past and in preparation for the future. Many years after the Passover in

Egypt, a person named John (*Yochanan*) the Baptist (Immerser), pointed to *Yeshua* and declared that He was the Lamb of G-d (John [*Yochanan*] 1:29). After John (*Yochanan*), a *type* of Elijah (*Eliyahu*) who would prepare the coming of Messiah, proclaimed *Yeshua* as the Lamb of G-d, *Yeshua* ministered for three-and-a-half years. At the end of that time, on the tenth of Nisan, the high priest marched out of the city of Jerusalem to Bethany where a lamb was to be slain. The lamb was led back into the city through streets lined with thousands of pilgrims singing the Hallel (Psalms [*Tehillim*] 113–118). The liturgy for *Hoshanah Rabbah* says that the Messiah will come to the Mount of Olives and weep over the city. This happened in Luke 19:41. The people also waved palm branches as *Yeshua* rode into the city on a donkey in fulfillment of Zechariah 9:9. Today, Nisan 10 is known as Palm Sunday in the non-Jewish community.

The lamb that was to be slain by the high priest was led into the temple (*Beit HaMikdash*) and put in a prominent place of display. Likewise, *Yeshua* the Lamb of G-d went on public display when He entered the temple (*Beit HaMikdash*) and spent four days there among the people, the Sadducees, the Pharisees, and the scribes, as the leaders asked *Yeshua* their hardest questions. *Yeshua* was questioned in front of the people for four days, showing Himself to be without spot or blemish, fulfilling Exodus (*Shemot*) 12:5.

On the fourteenth of Nisan, at the third hour of the day (9:00 a.m.), the high priest (*Cohen HaGadol*) took the lamb and ascended the altar so he could tie the lamb in place on the altar. At the same time on that day, *Yeshua* was tied to the tree on Mount Moriah (Mark 15:25). At the time of the evening sacrifice (3:00 p.m.) for Passover (Exodus [*Shemot*] 12:6), the high priest (*Cohen HaGadol*) ascended the altar, cut the throat of the lamb with a knife, and said the words, "It is finished." These are the exact words said after giving a peace offering to G-d. At this same time, *Yeshua* died, saying these exact words in John (*Yochanan*) 19:30. *Yeshua* died at exactly 3:00 p.m. (Matthew [*Mattityahu*] 27:45-46,50).

In Exodus (*Shemot*) 12:8-9, we are told the lamb was to be roasted before sundown. According to the tractate Pesahim in the Mishnah, the lamb was roasted on an upright pomegranate stick. This pomegranate stick is representative of the tree upon which *Yeshua* died. The lamb was to be gutted, and its intestines were to be removed and put over its head. Thus, the lamb is referred to as the "crowned sacrifice." This is a picture of *Yeshua* in (Psalm [*Tehillim*] 22:13-18).

Deuteronomy (*Devarim*) 16:16 says that all the congregation of Israel was required to be present at the feasts of Passover (*Pesach*), Weeks (*Shavuot*) or Pentecost, and Tabernacles (*Sukkot*). This explains why all were gathered to witness the death of *Yeshua* on the tree (Matthew [*Mattityahu*] 27:1-26).

The night of the fifteenth of Nisan, G-d commanded the people to eat the lamb with unleavened bread (*matzah*) and bitter herbs (*maror*), their sandals on their feet and their bags packed and on their backs (Exodus [*Shemot*] 12:6,8,11), for on this night they are to leave Egypt. Likewise, we are to be quick to accept *Yeshua* into our hearts and leave Egypt, which represents the sin and idolatry of this evil world.

The Feast of Passover in the Gospel of John

There are four recorded Passovers in the Gospel (*basar*) of John (*Yochanan*), even as *Yeshua* attended the Passover with His parents from year to year (Luke 2:41-42).

1. The first Passover *Yeshua* attended at Jerusalem (*Yerushalayim*) as an adult is recorded in John (*Yochanan*) 2:13-17. In these passages, He found the temple (*Beit HaMikdash*) defiled with money changers. He then declared that "My house shall be called of all nations the house of prayer..." (Mark 11:17). The spiritual application (*halacha*) is this: The believers in *Yeshua* are G-d's temple and we are not to defile it with sin (1 Corinthians 3:16-17; 2 Corinthians 6:14-18). Those who believe in the Messiah *Yeshua* are the house of G-d (Hebrews 3:6; 1 Timothy 3:15; 1 Peter [*Kefa*] 2:5).

2. The second Passover feast is recorded in John (*Yochanan*) 5:1-15. Although the particular feast is not specifically mentioned here, we know that it is either Passover (*Pesach*), Pentecost (*Shavuot*), or Tabernacles (*Sukkot*) because *Yeshua* went up (*aliyah*) to Jerusalem (*Yerushalayim*) to observe it (Deuteronomy [*Devarim*] 16:16). By knowing what *Yeshua* did in these passages and what these feasts teach us, the evidence suggests it was Passover. This Passover reveals *Yeshua* as the Healer of men's bodies and souls; the Forgiver of sin; and the Healer of disease. In the Egyptian Passover, Israel was to feed upon the body of the lamb. As they did, they were

saved from the destruction of Egypt and their bodies were healed (Exodus [*Shemot*] 12:13; Psalm [*Tehillim*] 105:26,36-37). Thus healing is associated with Passover, and at this Passover, *Yeshua* healed an impotent man.

3. The third Passover is found in John (*Yochanan*) 6:1-13. At Passover, the children of Israel ate the flesh of the lamb, sprinkled the blood on the door, and ate unleavened bread. Thus the bread and the lamb's body were eaten by all at Passover. In these passages, *Yeshua* is the Bread of Life, the unleavened bread, and the heavenly manna.

4. The fourth Passover is *Yeshua's* sacrificial death on the tree. He is the Lamb of G-d and the Unleavened Bread, dying despite having never sinned.

In the book of John (*Yochanan*) in the first Passover, *Yeshua* is the Temple Cleanser (the spiritual temple is the physical body of the believer). In the second Passover, *Yeshua* is the Healer of body and soul. In the third Passover, *Yeshua* is the Bread of Life. In the fourth Passover, *Yeshua* is the Lamb of G-d slain for the sins of the whole world.[3]

The Egyptian Redemption Is a Foreshadowing of the Messianic Redemption

The G-d of Israel's historical redemption of His people from Egypt is a type and foreshadowing of the *Messianic Redemption* in the end of days. Orthodox Jews call the regathering of *both houses* of Israel in the end of days the *Ingathering of the Exiles* or the *Messianic Redemption*. The

Ingathering of the Exiles/Messianic Redemption is a funda-mental and foundational belief of Orthodox Judaism. Ortho-dox Jews pray three times a day for the *Ingathering of the Exiles/Messianic Redemption*. The *Ingathering of the Exiles/ Messianic Redemption* is also one of the 13 articles of Jewish faith.

One of the many prophecies of the Ingathering of the Ex-iles/Messianic Redemption or the restoration of both houses of Israel in the writings of the prophets is found in Ezekiel (*Yechezekel*) 37:15-24 as it is written:

> *The word of the Lord came again unto me, saying, Moreover, thou son of man, take thee one stick, and write upon it, For Judah, and for the children of Israel his companions: then take another stick, and write upon it, For Joseph, the stick of Ephraim, and for all the house of Israel his companions: And join them one to another into one stick; and they shall become one in thine hand. And when the children of thy people shall speak unto thee, saying, Wilt thou not show us what thou meanest by these? Say unto them, Thus saith the Lord God; Behold, I will take the stick of Joseph, which is in the hand of Ephraim, and the tribes of Is-rael his fellows, and will put them with him, even with the stick of Judah, and make them one stick, and they shall be one in mine hand ... And say unto them, Thus saith the Lord God; Behold, I will take the children of Israel from among the heathen whither they have gone, and will gather them on every side, and bring them into their own land: And I will make them one nation in the land upon the mountains of Israel ...*

And David my servant shall be king over them; and they all shall have one shepherd: they shall also walk in my judgments, and observe my statutes and do them.

Who Is Ephraim/Joseph or the House of Israel?

According to Orthodox Jewish understanding of the end of days, Ephraim/Joseph or the *house of Israel* who is mentioned in the prophecy of Ezekiel (*Yechezekel*) 37:16,19 are the ten lost/scattered tribes from the Northern Kingdom of Israel who will be reunited with the Jewish people of the Southern Kingdom (*house of Judah*). The *Talmud* states in *Yebamot 16b-17a* that the ten tribes of the scattered Northern Kingdom in their places of exile in the end of days will be regarded as having the status of "Gentiles" (*goyim*) as far as keeping the Torah and *halacha* are concerned.

In the *Talmud* in Yebamot 16b it is written:

Rab Judah said in the name of R. Assi: If at the present time a heathen betroths [a daughter of Israel], note must be taken of such betrothal since it may be that he is of the ten tribes.

Therefore, Orthodox Judaism today views the ten lost/scattered tribes to be heathen or "Gentiles" (*goyim).*

However, the *halacha* (accepted belief of Orthodox Judaism) regarding the ten tribes of the scattered Northern Kingdom (*house of Israel*) is that they will in the end of days:

1. Embrace the Torah
2. Celebrate the Sabbath (*Shabbat*)

3. Observe the biblical festivals of Leviticus (*Vayikra*) 23
4. Reunite with the Southern Kingdom of Judah (*house of Judah*)
5. Return to the land of Israel (specifically the mountains of Israel or the West Bank) along with Judah prior to the coming of King Messiah (*Mashiach*).

Furthermore, there are Orthodox Jewish organizations today that are doing research to locate and identify the present descendents of the ten scattered tribes of the historical Northern Kingdom. Brit-Am (*Brit* in Hebrew = covenant and *Am* in Hebrew = people) founded by an Orthodox Jew named Yair Davidy who lives in Jerusalem, Israel, is one such organization. Based upon the biblical characteristics of the location of the ten scattered tribes in their exile in the end of days, history, archeological evidence and the traditional Orthodox Jewish perspective of the ten lost tribes based upon what is written about them in the *Talmud*, Yair Davidy has concluded that many of the present descendents of the ten scattered tribes of the Northern Kingdom are practicing the religion of Christianity. He has published these findings in several books that he has written and also in his ministry magazine.

What is fascinating about this Orthodox Jewish research is that, based upon careful examination of the writings in the New Testament (*Brit Hadashah*) including the words and teachings of *Yeshua*, the apostle Paul *(Rav Sha'ul)* and the apostle Peter (*Kefa*), the same conclusion can be drawn. When accepting *Yeshua* as Messiah (*Mashiach*), some of the descendents of the historical Northern Kingdom become a part of future Christianity.

The Northern Kingdom and the
New Testament *(Brit Hadashah)*

When they accept *Yeshua* as Messiah *(Mashiach)*, the New Testament *(Brit Hadashah)* links some of the historical descendents of the Northern Kingdom (ten scattered tribes) to Christianity. In Hosea *(Hoshea)* 1:9, the Northern Kingdom is called *lo-ammi* (not a people), but in Hosea *(Hoshea)* 1:10 they would be called in a future time *"sons of the living God"* and be reunited with the house of Judah in the end of days (Hosea [*Hoshea*] 1:11). The believers in *Yeshua* as Messiah *(Mashiach)* are linked with the prophecy of the destiny of the Northern Kingdom in Hosea *(Hoshea)* 1:9-10.

In First Peter *(Kefa)* 2:10, through belief in *Yeshua* as Messiah *(Mashiach)* those who were formerly called *lo-ammi* (not a people) are once again called *"sons of the living God."* Notice that this corresponds to the prophesied destiny of the Northern Kingdom based upon Hosea *(Hoshea)* 1:9-10.

In Romans chapters 9–11, the apostle Paul *(Rav Sha'ul)* links the "Gentiles" to the Northern Kingdom of Israel. In Romans 9:24, the apostle Paul *(Rav Sha'ul)* links the "Gentiles" with the prophecy of the Northern Kingdom in Hosea *(Hoshea)* 1:9-10, where those who were called *lo-ammi* (not a people) are now called *"children of the living God"* (Romans 9:25-26). In Romans 10:19, the apostle Paul *(Rav Sha'ul)* quotes from the Torah in Deuteronomy *(Devarim)* 32:21 where it prophesies that a future people who would become *"not a people"* would be used by the G-d of Israel to provoke Judah to jealousy. Finally in Romans 11:11, the apostle Paul (*Rav Sha'ul*) links those who were formerly *"not a people"* (the Northern Kingdom) as being "Gentiles" who would provoke Judah to jealousy in the end of days.

In Isaiah (*Yeshayahu*) 44:1-5, it was prophesied that when the G-d of Israel would outpour His Holy Spirit (*Ruach HaKodesh*) upon the descendents of Jacob in the end of days that they would *say* and subscribe/pledge allegiance that they are descendents (surnamed) from the house of Israel (Northern Kingdom).

Yeshua taught and linked His death on the tree to the purpose of regathering the lost sheep of the Northern Kingdom unto Him and their reuniting with the house of Judah in the end of days. In John (*Yochanan*) 10:14-19, *Yeshua* said that He is the "good shepherd." By making this statement, *Yeshua* is making an allusion to Ezekiel [*Yechezekel*] 34:11-15,23; 37:24 where the "good shepherd" would restore and reunite both houses of Israel. In John (*Yochanan*) 10:16, *Yeshua* said that He has other sheep (Northern Kingdom) who were not of the sheepfold of Judah (Southern Kingdom) for whom He would die and lay down His life so that there would be one sheepfold (John [*Yochanan*] 10:16; 11:52-53).

In first century Judaism there was an expectation from what is written in the Torah and the Prophets that the Messiah would reunite both houses of Israel (Isaiah [*Yeshayahu*] 49:5-6). For this reason, in Acts 1:6, *Yeshua* was asked by His disciples (*talmidim*) when He would restore the Kingdom to Israel (reunite both houses of Israel). *Yeshua* answered the question and said that both houses of Israel would be reunited through an outpouring of the Holy Spirit (*Ruach HaKodesh*). He also said that the message of the restoration and reunification of both houses of Israel would be preached in all the world as a witness (Acts 1:8). The apostle Paul (*Rav Sha'ul*) also preached the message of the restoration of both houses of Israel in Acts 26:6-7.

The Messianic Redemption Is Like the Egyptian Redemption

The prophets of Israel teach us that this outpouring of the Holy Spirit (*Ruach HaKodesh*) to gather both houses of Israel will happen in the end of days prior to the coming of King Messiah (*Mashiach*). This began in Acts 2 on the day of Pentecost (*Shavuot*) and culminates in the end of days when *Yeshua* will reign over both houses of Israel (House of Jacob, Luke 1:33) during the Messanic Era. The prophets of Israel liken the future redemption of both houses of Israel to the historical Egyptian redemption but on a global scale. In Micah (*Michah*) 7:15 it is written:

> *According to the days of thy coming out of the land of Egypt will I show unto him marvelous things.*

In Hosea (Hoshea) 2:14-15 it is written:

> *Therefore, behold, I will allure her, and bring her into the wilderness, and speak comfortably unto her. And I will give her her vineyards from thence, and the valley of Achor [trouble] for a door of hope: and she shall sing there, as in the days of her youth, and as in the day when she came up out of the land of Egypt.*

In Ezekiel (*Yechezekel*) 20:34-36 it is written:

And I will bring you out from the people, and will gather you out of the countries wherein ye are scattered, with a mighty hand, and with a stretched out arm [historical Passover language], *and with fury poured out. And I will bring you into the wilderness of the people, and there will I plead with you face to face.* **Like as I pleaded with your fathers in the wilderness of the land of Egypt,** *so will I plead with you, saith the Lord God.*

All Believers in *Yeshua* Have Been Redeemed From Egypt

When doing a Passover Seder, you are supposed to see yourself as if you are personally being redeemed from Egypt. In Exodus (*Shemot*) 13:8, it is commanded that you shall show your son "in that day [future] saying, This is done because of that which the Lord did unto me [past] when I [personally] came forth out of Egypt." In First Corinthians 10:1-4, the apostle Paul (*Rav Sha'ul*) reminds the followers of *Yeshua* as Messiah (*Mashiach*) to have the mindset that they and their fathers were redeemed from Egypt. In Exodus (*Shemot*) 15:1 it says, "Then sang Moses and the children of Israel" and said "I *will sing*" (future). This reminds us that there will be a *future redemption* to come that will be like the historical Egyptian redemption. Those redeemed in this future redemption will sing the song of Moses and the song of the Lamb (Revelation 15:3).

For a greater understanding of this future *Ingathering of the Exiles/Messianic Redemption* or the restoration of both houses of Israel (members of Christianity and Judaism) in the end of days, I would encourage you to read the book that I've written on this subject entitled, *Restoring the Two Houses of Israel.* Information on how to order the two houses of Israel book and the other book that I've written entitled, *Who Is the Bride of Christ?*, is given at the end of this book.

The Conclusion of Passover (Pesach)

In concluding our study of Passover (*Pesach*), we can see that the G-d of Israel gave Passover (*Pesach*) to His people so we could understand the death of *Yeshua* on the tree during His first coming, as well as understand our personal spiritual salvation in *Yeshua* from Pharaoh and Egypt (who are likened to satan [*ha satan*] and the kingdom of sin and darkness). Furthermore, the historical Egyptian Passover was also given by the G-d of Israel so we could understand the future redemption of His people (both houses of Israel who are today called by the corporate names of Christianity and Judaism) in the end of days when they will return to the land of Israel (specifically, the mountains of Israel or the West Bank). This redemption will take place in the end of days prior to the coming of King Messiah (*Mashiach*). Because of the historical deliverance from the bondage of Egypt, our personal salvation in *Yeshua* as Messiah (*Mashiach*) and our future redemption from exile in the nations of the world and return to the land of Israel in the end of days, Passover (*Pesach*) has been given by the rabbis the appropriate title of the "Feast of our Freedom!!!"

Chapter 4

The Festival of Unleavened Bread (*Hag HaMatzah*)

The Feast of Unleavened Bread (*Hag HaMatzah*) is the fifteenth day of the month of Nisan, which is the day following Passover (*Pesach*). It is a seven-day festival to the L-rd (Leviticus [*Vayikra*] 23:6-7; Exodus [*Shemot*] 12:7-8,14-17). On the fifteenth of Nisan and for the next seven days, G-d forbade the people to have any leavened bread in their houses.

The festival of Unleavened Bread can be found in Exodus (*Shemot*) 12:14-17, as it is written:

Now this day will be a memorial to you, and you shall celebrate it as a feast to the Lord; throughout your generations you are to celebrate it as a permanent ordinance. Seven days you shall eat unleavened bread, but on the first day you shall remove leaven from your houses; for whoever eats anything leavened from the first day until the seventh day, that person shall be cut off from Israel. And on the first day you shall have a

*holy assembly, and another holy assembly on the sev-
enth day; no work at all shall be done on them, except
what must be eaten by every person, that alone may be
prepared by you. You shall also observe the Feast of
Unleavened Bread, for on this very day I brought your
hosts out of the land of Egypt; therefore you shall observe this day throughout your generations as a permanent ordinance* (Exodus [*Shemot*] 12:14-17 NAS).

The Book of Exodus (*Shemot*), chapter 12, describes the
Egyptian Passover. After the lamb was killed, the blood was
to be put on the doorposts. The lamb was to be roasted in fire
and eaten with *matzah* (unleavened bread) and bitter herbs
(Exodus [*Shemot*] 12:7-8).

Purging Leaven From the House (*Bedikat HaMetz*)

G-d gave a ceremony of searching and removing leaven
from the house prior to the festival of Unleavened Bread in
preparation for the festival. In Hebrew, this ceremony is
called *Bedikat HaMetz*, which means "the search for
leaven." The ceremony is as follows:

The preparation for searching and removing the leaven
(*Bedikat HaMetz*) from the house actually begins before Passover (*Pesach*). First, the wife thoroughly cleans the house to
remove all leaven (*HaMetz*) from it. In the Bible, leaven
(*HaMetz*) is symbolic of sin.

Spiritual Application (*Halacha*). Spiritually, the believers in the Messiah *Yeshua* are the house of G-d (Hebrews
3:6; 1 Peter 2:5; 1 Timothy 3:15; Ephesians 2:19). Leaven
(sin) is to be cleaned out of our house, which is our body
(1 Corinthians 3:16-17; 6:19-20; 2 Corinthians 6:15-18).

In cleaning the house, the wife is instructed to purposely leave ten small pieces of leaven (bread) in the house. Then the father takes the children, along with a candle, a wooden spoon, a feather, and a piece of linen cloth, and searches through the house for the ten pieces of leaven. By nightfall on the day before Passover (*Pesach*), a final and comprehensive search is performed. At this time, the house is completely dark except for the candles. Once the father finds the leaven (bread), he sets the candle down by the leaven and lays the wooden spoon beside the leaven. Then he uses the feather to sweep the leaven onto the spoon. Without touching the leaven, he takes the feather, spoon, and leaven, wraps them in a linen cloth, and casts them out of the door of the house. The next morning (the fourteenth of Nisan), he goes into the synagogue and puts the linen cloth and its contents into a fire to be burned.

***Spiritual Application* (*Halacha*).** Spiritually, we are to cleanse the leaven (sin) from our houses (lives) by allowing the Holy Spirit (*Ruach HaKodesh*) to reveal to us, through the knowledge of *Yeshua* and the Scriptures, the sin that is in our lives. It is only through G-d's Word that we are able to identify sin in our lives as it is written in Psalm (*Tehillim*) 119:105, "Thy word is a lamp unto my feet, and a light unto my path." So the spiritual understanding of the candle is that it represents the Word of G-d. The feather represents the Holy Spirit (*Ruach HaKodesh*). Even though we have the Word of G-d, we need the Spirit of G-d (*Ruach HaKodesh*) to illuminate the entire Bible to us, including the Torah and the Tanach (1 Corinthians 2:11-14).

***Messianic Fulfillment*.** The spoon represents the tree that *Yeshua* died upon (Deuteronomy [*Devarim*] 21:22-23). The leaven (*HaMetz*) (sin) was swept on the spoon (the tree) as part of the ceremony. Likewise, our sin was swept or cast upon *Yeshua* (2 Corinthians 5:21) when *Yeshua* died upon the tree. The leaven (*Yeshua* upon the tree) was then wrapped in linen and *Yeshua* was cast out of His house (His body) and went to hell, which is a place of burning (Luke 16:19-24). Thus He fulfilled the part of the ceremony where the father takes the linen cloth and its contents and casts it into the fire to be burned.[1]

The Fifteenth of Nisan—Purging Out of Sin

The fifteenth of Nisan (*Hag HaMatzah*) marks the beginning of a seven-day feast period when Israel was to eat bread without leaven (sin) in remembrance of their baking unleavened bread in their haste to escape Egypt. The primary theme of this feast is the purging out of leaven (sin). Historically, there are two notable events that happened on this day.

1. **The Exodus journey beginning from Egypt** (Exodus [*Shemot*] 12:41). In Deuteronomy (*Devarim*) 16:3, the bread is referred to as "the bread of affliction."

2. **The burial of *Yeshua* after His crucifixion, who is the Bread of Life** (John [*Yochanan*] 6:35). In fact, the place of *Yeshua's* birth, Bethlehem, comes from two Hebrew words, *beit* and *lechem*. *Beit* means "house" and *lechem* means "bread." So, Bethlehem means house of bread. Therefore, *Yeshua*, who is the Bread of G-d, was born at a place called the house of bread.[2]

The festivals are fixed appointments (*mo'ed*) of G-d specifying what He will perform and the exact time He will perform it. The Jews had to hurry to put *Yeshua's* body in the ground because the sabbath was drawing near. This sabbath was a high sabbath and the first day of Unleavened Bread (Nisan 15). This can be found in (John [*Yochanan*] 19:31). This would mean that *Yeshua* died on the fourteenth of Nisan, the day of Passover. *Yeshua* was in the sepulcher the day following His crucifixion, which was the fifteenth of Nisan, the first day of Unleavened Bread.

The Messianic Understanding of the *Matzah* in the Passover Seder

One of the 15 steps during the Passover Seder is a step called *Yachatz*. *Yachatz* is when the middle of the three *matzot* is broken into two. During the Passover Seder, there is a bag called the *matzatosh* which contains three pieces of *matzot*. The middle piece of *matzot* is removed, broken, wrapped in linen, and buried. This piece of *matzah* is the *afikomen*. During this part of the service, the *afikomen* was removed from sight (this represented *Yeshua* being buried) and it remained hidden until later in the service. *Yeshua* is the bread that was buried because He is the Bread of Life who came down from Heaven (John [*Yochanan*] 6:35). *Yeshua* was removed from between the two thieves who were crucified with Him (Matthew [*Mattityahu*] 27:38), wrapped in linen, and buried in the earth (Matthew 27:59-60).

Toward the end of the Passover Seder, the twelfth step to the service is called *Tzafun*. During *Tzafun*, the *afikomen* that was previously buried is redeemed and ransomed. At this point in the service, the *matzah*, previously characterized as the bread of affliction, is now transformed and redeemed. This is a perfect picture of *Yeshua*, who fulfilled the role of the suffering Messiah known as Messiah ben Yosef. He suffered affliction while dying on the tree, but was later redeemed when He was resurrected by G-d the Father. In the Passover Seder service, the *afikomen* is redeemed by the children. The children who find the buried *afikomen* receive a gift. This gift is known as the promise of the father. Likewise, when G-d resurrected *Yeshua* after He was buried in the earth, those who believed upon Him by faith (*emunah*) are given gifts by G-d. When *Yeshua* ascended to Heaven, He gave gifts to men (Ephesians 4:7-8). These gifts included righteousness (Romans 5:17-18), eternal life (Romans 6:23), grace (Romans 5:12,14-15), faith (Ephesians 2:8-9), and other spiritual gifts (1 Corinthians 12:1,4). Some other gifts include wisdom, knowledge, healing, the working of miracles, prophecy, the discerning of spirits, tongues, and interpretation of tongues (1 Corinthians 12:8-11), in addition to the gifts of helps and administration (1 Corinthians 12:28).[3]

The Feast of Unleavened Bread in the Bible

1. **The Feast of Unleavened Bread was so much a part of Passover (*Pesach*) that the names of Passover and Unleavened Bread were used interchangeably or almost synonymously** (Luke 22:1).

2. **The feast was to be kept seven days** (Exodus [*Shemot*] 12:15-19). The number seven is the biblical number for completion or fullness. The believer who keeps this feast is to keep it fully unto the L-rd and set himself aside completely to Him. The Feast of Unleavened Bread speaks of complete separation from all things that

are leavened (sinful) and feeding upon *Yeshua*, who is the believer's bread (John [*Yochanan*] 6:32-36,38).

3. **The Feast of Unleavened Bread (*Hag HaMatzah*) is a high sabbath day.** A high sabbath in Hebrew is called a *shabbaton*. During Passover, there is an extra sabbath besides the weekly sabbath. These sabbaths are called high sabbaths. The high sabbath of Unleavened Bread can be seen in John 19:31.

4. **Unleavened bread is used for consecration and separation.** It is also anointed with oil. The believers in the Messiah *Yeshua* are to be consecrated and separated to do the work G-d has called us to do and to live a life that is holy to Him. If we do this, the anointing of the Holy Spirit (*Ruach HaKodesh*) of G-d will rest upon our lives.

    a. The bread represents consecration (Leviticus [*Vayikra*] 8:1-2,26–27; Exodus [*Shemot*] 29:2-23).

    b. It was included in the sacred vow of separation of the Nazarites (Numbers [*Bamidbar*] 6:1-21).

    c. It was the food for the priests in the meal and peace offering (Leviticus [*Vayikra*] 2:1,4,14-16; 6:14-18; 7:11-12).

    d. It marked Israel's divine separation from Egypt's (the world's) life of slavery and bondage (Exodus [*Shemot*] 12:17,30-34).

    e. All leaven was to be put away (Exodus [*Shemot*] 12:15,19-20). When leaven or yeast is placed in an unleavened batch of dough, the leaven puffs up the dough. Likewise, when we allow sin into our lives, it will puff us up in pride and arrogance.[4]

In the Bible, G-d referred to the leaven of different groups of people. These are listed as follows:

1. **The leaven of Herod** (Mark 8:14-15; 6:14-18; Matthew [*Mattityahu*] 2:7-12).

2. **The leaven of the Pharisees** (Mark 8:15; Matthew [*Mattityahu*] 16:5-12; 23:1-3; Luke 11:37-44; 12:1).

3. **The leaven of the Sadducees** (Matthew [*Mattityahu*] 16:6-12). The Sadducees did not believe in the supernatural. They denied the existence of the Spirit of G-d, angels, and the resurrection (Mark 12:18; Acts 23:6-8).

4. **The leaven at Corinth**. The leaven at Corinth was sensuality, chiefly fornication (1 Corinthians 4:17-21; 5:1-13; 6:1,9-11,13,16-18; 8:1; 13:4; 2 Corinthians 12:20-21).

How to Keep the Feast

Spiritual Application (Halacha). Spiritually, the feast is kept in sincerity and truth. Sincerity involves purity and serving G-d with a pure heart. It involves putting away the sin in our lives, and separating ourselves from all evil that has a corrupting influence in the life of the believer in *Yeshua*. Historically, Israel learned that keeping the feast meant a complete separation from Egypt's religion, bondage, food, and slavery, as well as its worldly glory, wisdom, and splendor.

The children of Israel took the dough before it was leavened because they could not tarry in Egypt. There was no time to let the leaven get in and work up the dough (Exodus 12:34,39). As believers, we are to flee the world's ways and philosophies that are contrary to the Word of G-d. Sincerity (1 Corinthians 5:7-8) involves purity and sanctification, which means holiness and separation. The Bible uses water and washing to instruct us concerning sanctification and separation (Joshua 24:14; Ephesians 5:26; 6:24; Philippians 1:10; 1 Peter 2:2). To sanctify means to make holy, to purify, or to consecrate. The believers are sanctified by obeying the entire Word of G-d, including the Torah and the Tanach (John 17:17,19; Acts 20:32; 2 Chronicles 30:15; 35:1,6; Exodus 19:10,14; 28:39-41; Leviticus 8:30; 11:44; 20:7; Hebrews 10:10,14; 1 Corinthians 1:2).

In First Corinthians 6:11, sanctification is connected to washing (Acts 22:16). Historically, after Israel celebrated the Passover, they were immersed (washed) in the water of the Red Sea (1 Corinthians 10:1-2). Likewise, after we accept the Messiah into our lives, we must immerse ourselves in studying the Bible and, by so doing, enable the knowledge of the Word of G-d to transform and change our lives.

Chapter 5

The Festival of First Fruits (*Bikkurim*)

The fifteenth of Nisan begins *Hag HaMatzah* (the Feast of Unleavened Bread), which is a high sabbath, a *shabbaton*. It is a seven-day feast to the L-rd. The day following the sabbath during Passover is called the Feast of First Fruits (Leviticus [*Vayikra*] 23:10-11).

The Feast of First Fruits can be found in Leviticus (*Vayikra*) 23:9-14, as it is written:

Then the Lord spoke to Moses, saying, "Speak to the sons of Israel, and say to them, 'When you enter the land which I am going to give to you and reap its harvest, then you shall bring in the sheaf of the first fruits of your harvest to the priest. And he shall wave the sheaf before the Lord for you to be accepted; on the day after the sabbath the priest shall wave it. Now on the day when you wave the sheaf, you shall offer a male lamb one year old without defect for a burnt offering to the Lord. Its grain offering shall then be two-tenths of an ephah of fine flour mixed with oil, an offering by fire to the Lord for a soothing aroma, with its libation, a fourth of a hin of wine. Until this same day, until you have brought in the offering of your God, you shall eat neither bread nor roasted grain nor new growth. It is to be a perpetual statute throughout your generations in all your dwelling places' " (Leviticus [*Vayikra*] 23:9-14 NAS).

Understanding the Festival Ceremony

The observance was carried out in this manner, when the standing ripe harvest of barley and wheat was ready to be reaped. The celebrant would take one sheaf from the standing harvest and bring it to the priest. The lone sheaf was called "the sheaf of the first fruits." The priest was then to take this one sheaf and wave it before the L-rd in His house. This was to be done "the day after the sabbath." Prescribed offerings were also to be presented along with the sheaf.[1]

The Sheaf of First Fruits in the Bible

G-d commanded the people to bring a sheaf of the harvest (Leviticus [*Vayikra*] 23:10). The Hebrew word for "sheaf" is *omer*. An *omer* is defined as "a measure of dry things, containing a tenth part of an ephah." The definition of an *omer* being a tenth part of an ephah is found in Exodus (*Shemot*) 16:36. An ephah contains 10 *omers* of grain. Remember, three times a year G-d commanded the people to come to Jerusalem (*Yerushalayim*) to celebrate the festivals of Passover (*Pesach*), Pentecost (*Shavuot*), and Tabernacles (*Sukkot*). All three of these festivals are agricultural harvest festivals. Passover (*Pesach*) is the barley harvest. Pentecost (*Shavuot*) is the wheat harvest. Both of these festivals are first fruits harvests before the final harvest that was to come at the end of the year during the festival of Tabernacles (*Sukkot*), which is the fruit harvest.

The harvest represents all who would put their faith, trust, and confidence (*emunah*) in the Messiah *Yeshua* (Matthew [*Mattityahu*] 13:39; Mark 4:26-29; Luke 10:1-12; Revelation 14:14-16). So, the sheaf is the first of the first fruits. Since a sheaf in the Bible is used to typify a person or persons (Genesis [*Bereishit*] 37:5-11), a sheaf spiritually represents people who accept the Messiah into their hearts.

The nation of Israel was familiar with the concept of first fruits or the firstborn. The first fruits were always the choicest, the foremost, the first, the best, the preeminent of all that was to follow. They were holy to the L-rd. The concept of first fruits or firstborn is a major theme in the Bible. This can be seen by the following Scriptures: Exodus (*Shemot*) 23:16,19: 34:26; Leviticus (*Vayikra*) 2:12,14; 23:20; Numbers (*Bamidbar*) 18:12-15,26; Deuteronomy (*Devarim*) 18:1-5; 26:2-4,10; 2 Chronicles 31:5; Nehemiah 10:35-39; Proverbs (*Mishlai*) 3:9; Jeremiah (*Yermiyahu*) 2:3; Ezekiel (*Yechezekel*) 44:30; 48:14; Malachi 3:8-14; Hebrews 6:20; 7:1-8.

Everything on the earth, both man and beast, was to be presented before the L-rd as first fruits to Him.

1. The firstborn of both man and beast were sanctified (made holy) and presented to the L-rd (Exodus [*Shemot*] 13:2; 22:29).

2. The first fruits of all the earth were presented to the L-rd at His altar in praise and thanksgiving (Deuteronomy [*Devarim*] 26:1-11).[2]

The Seventeenth of Nisan—Resurrection and Salvation

The theme of the festival of First Fruits is resurrection and salvation. There are several important events that happened on this day in the Bible.

1. **Noah's (*Noach*) ark rests on Mount Ararat** (Genesis 8:4).

2. **Israel crosses the Red Sea** (Exodus [*Shemot*] 3:18; 5:3,14).

3. **Israel eats the first fruits of the Promised Land** (Joshua 5:10-12). The manna that G-d gave from Heaven during the days in the wilderness ceased the sixteenth day of Nisan after the people ate of the old corn of the land. The day following was the seventeenth of Nisan, the day when the children of Israel ate the first fruits of the Promised Land.[3]

4. **Haman is defeated**[4] (Esther 3:1-6). In the Book of Esther, Haman plotted to kill all the Jews in Persia and Media. Haman had ten sons (Esther 9:12). By this, we can see that Haman is a type of the false Messiah (antichrist). A decree was sent out on the thirteenth of Nisan that all the Jews would be killed (Esther 3:12). Upon hearing this news, Esther proclaims a three-day fast, which would be Nisan 14-16 (Esther 4:16). On the sixteenth of Nisan, Esther risked her life when she came to King Ahasuerus. The king asked her, in effect, "Tell me, what do you want?" Esther said, "If it please the king,

may the king and Haman come this day to the banquet that I have prepared for him" (Esther 5:4 NAS). This was the sixteenth day of Nisan. At the banquet, the king again asked Esther what she wanted, and she asked the king to come to another banquet to be held the next day, the seventeenth of Nisan. On this day, Haman (a type of the false Messiah or antichrist, as well as of satan [*Ha satan*]) is hanged.

5. **The resurrection of *Yeshua*, the Messiah** (John 12:24; 1 Corinthians 15:16-20). *Yeshua* celebrated the festival of First Fruits by offering Himself as the first fruits to all future generations (Matthew [*Mattityahu*] 27:52-53).

Yeshua Is the First Fruits of the Barley Harvest

1. *Yeshua* **is the firstborn of *Miryam* (Mary)** (Matthew 1:23-25).

2. *Yeshua* **is the first-begotten of G-d the Father** (Hebrews 1:6).

3. *Yeshua* **is the firstborn of every creature** (Colossians 1:15).

4. *Yeshua* **is the first-begotten from the dead** (Revelation 1:5).

5. *Yeshua* **is the firstborn of many brethren** (Romans 8:29).

6. *Yeshua* **is the first fruits of the resurrected ones** (1 Corinthians 15:20,23).

7. *Yeshua* **is the beginning of the creation of G-d** (Revelation 3:14).

8.   *Yeshua* is the preeminent One (Colossians 1:18).[5]

Yeshua is indeed the Most Holy One of G-d and is sanctified by the Father. *Yeshua* is the first, the choicest, the preeminent One. He is both the firstborn of G-d and the first fruits unto G-d. *Yeshua* is the sheaf of the first fruits.

First Fruits Is Prophetic
of the Resurrection of the Messiah

The festival of the sheaf of the first fruits is prophetic of the resurrection of *Yeshua*. *Yeshua* prophesied that He would rise three days and nights after He was slain on the tree (Matthew [*Mattityahu*] 12:38-40; 16:21; Luke 24:44-46). This was foreshadowed to happen in the Tanach (Old Testament) by type and shadow (Genesis [*Bereishit*] 22:1-6; Exodus [*Shemot*] 3:18; 5:3; 8:27; Esther 4:15-17; Jonah 1:7; 2:1-2).

Since *Yeshua* was slain on the tree on the day of Passover (*Pesach*), the fourteenth of Nisan, and He arose from the grave three days and nights after He was slain, *Yeshua* arose from the grave on the seventeenth of Nisan, the day of the festival of First Fruits. In fact, *Yeshua* is called the first fruits of those who rise from the dead.

> *But now Christ has been raised from the dead, the first fruits of those who are asleep. For since by a man came death, by a man also came the resurrection of the dead. For as in Adam all die, so also in Christ all shall be made alive. But each in his own order: Christ the first fruits, after that those who are Christ's at His coming* (1 Corinthians 15:20-23 NAS).

It was prophesied that *Yeshua*, the Messiah, would be buried in the tomb of the rich (Isaiah [*Yeshayahu*] 53:9; Matthew [*Mattityahu*] 27:57; Luke 23:51). Why was *Yeshua* placed in the tomb of Joseph of Arimathaea? Arimathaea was another name for Ramah, where Samuel dwelt. It is five miles north of Jerusalem (*Yerushalayim*). This place is still called Ramah today. In ancient times, it was customary for Jews to be buried in Jerusalem (*Yerushalayim*). In fact, this practice is still done today because it is a traditional belief in Judaism that the resurrection of the dead will take place in Jerusalem (*Yerushalayim*) first.

In the Book of Genesis (*Bereishit*), Joseph (*Yosef*) the son of Jacob (*Ya'akov*), made the children of Israel take a vow that when they went to the Promised Land, they would carry his bones with them (Genesis [*Bereishit*] 50:24-26). Ramah was a term that represented idolatry. Two countries were called the seat of idolatry in the ancient world: Babylon and Egypt. Joseph (*Yosef*), the son of Jacob (*Ya'akov*), was also known as Joseph of Ramah. Moses (*Moshe*) took the bones of Joseph (*Yosef*) with him when he and the children of Israel journeyed to Succoth (Exodus [*Shemot*] 13:19-20). Therefore, Joseph's (*Yosef*) tomb in Egypt was empty. The empty tomb of Joseph (*Yosef*) of Arimathaea (Ramah), which stood for wickedness, was a fulfillment of Isaiah (*Yeshayahu*) 53:9.[6]

Joseph (*Yosef*) was a type of the role of *Yeshua* during His first coming when He came to fulfill the role of the suffering Messiah known as Messiah ben Joseph. The bones of Joseph (*Yosef*) were carried to Succoth. Succoth is a type of the Messianic age also known as the Millennium. This is also a picture of *Yeshua* being both Messiah ben Joseph and Messiah ben David—as *Yeshua* who suffered during His first coming to earth will be King during His second coming to earth.

The Spiritual Understanding of First Fruits

Spiritual Application (Halacha). A sheaf in the Bible is used to typify a person or persons (Genesis [*Bereishit*] 37:5-11). *Yeshua* will return to earth (Zechariah 14:4) during His second coming as King over all the earth. He also will bring the sheaves (the believers in *Yeshua* as the Messiah) with Him (Psalm [*Tehillim*] 126; Jeremiah [*Yermiyahu*] 31:9-14; Joel 3:11-13; Zechariah 14:3-5; Matthew [*Mattityahu*] 13:37-39; Mark 4:26-29; Hebrews 12:1; Jude 14; Revelation 1:7).

The 144,000 witnesses of *Yeshua* from the tribes of Israel during the *Chevlai shel Mashiach*, the birthpangs of the Messiah (also known as the tribulation) are first fruits to G-d during the tribulation period (Revelation 14:1-4).

Let's look at some Scriptures in the Bible concerning first fruits.

1. **The natural is before the spiritual** (1 Corinthians 15:46).

2. **Israel was G-d's firstborn** (Exodus [*Shemot*] 4:22). But, the first will be last and the last will be first (Mark 10:31). Therefore, the Gentiles (the *goyim*) became the first to receive the Messiah (as a corporate people; there are many non-Jews who do not) (Isaiah [*Yeshayahu*] 60:1-3; 62:1-3; Acts 15:14-16). At the end of this present age, the Jews as a corporate people will accept *Yeshua* as Messiah as well.

3. **The gospel (*basar*) was preached to the Jew first and then to the non-Jews** (Romans 1:16; 2:9-10; Matthew [*Mattityahu*] 10:5-6; 15:21-28; Acts 1:8).

4. **We are called to seek first the Kingdom of G-d** (Matthew [*Mattityahu*] 6:33).

5. *Yeshua* **was the first to rise from the dead** (Acts 26:23).

6. **The early believers were a kind of first fruits** (James [*Ya'akov*] 1:17-18).

7. **Those who arose from the dead with *Yeshua* during His resurrection became the first fruits of all those who would rise from the dead** (Matthew [*Mattityahu*] 27:52-53; Ephesians 4:8; 1 Thessalonians 4:13-18).

8. *Yeshua* **first loved us, and He is to be our first love** (1 John [*Yochanan*] 4:9; Revelation 2:4).

9. *Yeshua* **is the first (*Aleph*) and the last (*Tav*)** (Revelation 1:8,11,17; 22:13; Isaiah [*Yeshayahu*] 41:4; 44:6; 48:12).

Chapter 6

The Festival of Pentecost (*Shavuot*)

And you shall celebrate the Feast of Weeks, that is, the first fruits of the wheat harvest… (Exodus [*Shemot*] 34:22 NAS).

You shall count seven weeks for yourself; you shall begin to count seven weeks from the time you begin to put the sickle to the standing grain. Then you shall celebrate the Feast of Weeks to the Lord your God with a tribute of a freewill offering of your hand, which you shall give just as the Lord your God blesses you (Deuteronomy [*Devarim*] 16:9-10 NAS).

The *Omer*: Countdown to Sinai

The period called "the *omer*" begins the day following the sabbath during Passover (*Pesach*) and continues until *Shavuot* (Pentecost). The Torah commanded that seven weeks be counted from the time of the offering of the *omer*, as it says:

You shall also count for yourselves from the day after the sabbath, from the day when you brought in the

*sheaf of the wave offering; there shall be seven com-
plete [temimot] sabbaths. You shall count fifty days to
the day after the seventh sabbath; then you shall present a new grain offering to the Lord. You shall bring
in from your dwelling places two loaves of bread for a
wave offering.... . On this same day you shall make a
proclamation as well; you are to have a holy convocation. You shall do no laborious work. It is to be a perpetual statute in all your dwelling places throughout
your generations* (Leviticus [*Vayikra*] 23:15-17,21
NAS).

Because of this ritual of counting, the period between
Passover (*Pesach*) and Pentecost (*Shavuot*) came to be
known as the *omer*. In fact, *Shavuot* does not have a fixed
calendar date in the Bible, but rather falls on the day after the
completion of the *omer* count—that is, the fiftieth day after
the *omer* offering is brought.[1]

The Ceremony of Counting the *Omer*

A sharp controversy existed between the rabbis and a va-
riety of Jewish sects over the interpretation of the words "the
day after the sabbath" in the verse commanding the counting
of the *omer*. According to the rabbis, the sabbath refers not to
the weekly sabbath, but rather to the first festival day of the
Passover (*Pesach*). [This is Nisan 15, the first day of Unleavened Bread, which G-d designated to be a high sabbath
(*shabbaton*). Because of this, the counting of the *omer* traditionally begins from Nisan 15.] Various groups, beginning
with the first-century Sadducees and continuing with the
Karaites of the early Middle Ages, interpreted the word *sabbath* to mean the weekly sabbath during the Passover (*Pesach*)

season. The implication of this interpretation is that *Shavuot* (Pentecost), which falls on the day after the *omer* count of 49 days, would always occur on a Sunday. Before the counting of the *omer*, this blessing is recited: "Praised are You, L-rd our G-d, Ruler of the Universe who has sanctified us with His commandments, commanding us to count the omer." This is followed by the count for the day: "Today is the first day of the omer." Weeks are counted as well. For example: "Today is the seventeenth day of the omer, which equals two weeks and three days of the omer." This counting is done at night, as the new day begins at sundown (6:00 p.m.). Some people recite Psalm (*Tehillim*) 67 after the counting, since it consists of seven verses and a total of 49 words in Hebrew.[2]

The Historical Understanding of Pentecost (*Shavuot*)

In the third month after the Jews left Egypt (*Mitzrayim*), they arrived in the Sinai desert and camped opposite Mount Sinai. Moses (*Moshe*) was then told by G-d to gather the Israelites together to receive the Torah (Exodus [*Shemot*] 19:1-8 NAS). The Israelites answered, "All that the Lord has spoken we will do!" In Hebrew, it is *Na'aseh V'Nishmah*, which means, "We agree to do even before we have listened."

Moses (*Moshe*) then gave the Jews two days to cleanse themselves, wash their clothes, and prepare to receive the Torah on the third day. At the same time, Moses (*Moshe*) told them not to come too near Mount Sinai. From early morning, dense clouds covered the peak of the mountain. Thunder and lightning were frequently seen and heard. The sound of the *shofar* (ram's horn) came very strong, and the top of the mountain was enveloped in fire and smoke. The Israelites at the foot of Mount Sinai stood in great awe (Exodus [*Shemot*] 19:9-19). Moses (*Moshe*) then went up alone on the mountain, and as he neared the top, a mighty voice announced the Ten Commandments (Exodus [*Shemot*] 19:20-25; 20:1-21).[3]

Later Development of the Holiday

Pentecost (*Shavuot*) traditionally has been seen in different ways. One is to see it as the concluding piece of the Passover (*Pesach*) season. The other is to see it as an independent festival. Because Pentecost (*Shavuot*) celebrates the revelation of G-d at Mount Sinai, Pentecost (*Shavout*) would seem to be of a clearly independent nature. It is, after all, counted as one of the three pilgrimage festivals (Deuteronomy [*Devarim*] 16:16). Yet, beginning with the Targum (the Aramaic translation of the Scriptures from the second century of the Christian Era or Common Era (C.E.), known more commonly as A.D.), Pentecost (*Shavuot*) is referred to in the rabbinic tradition as *Atzeret*. The word *atzeret* in Hebrew means "conclusion." The word *atzeret* is used in the Bible with the festival *Shemini Atzeret* (Numbers [*Bamidbar*] 29:35) and seems to mean "remain with Me [G-d] another day." There is a sense, therefore, that *atzeret* is the final part or completion of a festival. Therefore, *Shavuot* (Pentecost) is seen as the conclusion to the Passover (*Pesach*) season. One strong connection between Passover (*Pesach*) and *Shavuot* (Pentecost) is the counting of the *omer* serving as a chain that links the two festivals.[4]

Spiritual Application (Halacha). Because *Shavuot* (Pentecost) culminates with the counting of the *omer* for 50 days, *Shavuot* (Pentecost) is called the *Atzeret* or conclusion to

Passover (*Pesach*). Spiritually speaking (*halacha*), the believers in the Messiah *Yeshua* are on a journey out of Egypt (a type of the world's system and its evil ways) in the wilderness (of life), awaiting our time to meet G-d face to face on Mount Sinai (Exodus [*Shemot*] 3:12). There at Mount Sinai (spiritually), G-d will forever reveal Himself to us in a new and greater way. For all believers in the Messiah *Yeshua*, the Torah that was given at Mount Sinai represents the Word of G-d, the entire Bible. The believer in *Yeshua* spiritually experiences *Shavuot* (Pentecost) when the Holy Spirit of G-d (*Ruach HaKodesh*) reveals the Word of G-d to him in a deeper and more powerful way, and his understanding and desire for the Bible increases accordingly.

Themes of *Shavuot* (Pentecost)

New Revelation

One theme of *Shavuot* (Pentecost) is a new revelation of G-d's will (Leviticus [*Vayikra*] 23:15-16,21). Two notable historical events happened on this day.

1. **The giving of the Ten Commandments or the Torah.** It should be noted here that the Hebrew word *Torah*, commonly translated as "law" in English, does not mean "law," but "instruction or teaching" in the Hebrew language. By understanding the meaning of the Hebrew word *Torah,* we can see that the Torah was *never* intended, nor should it ever be understood by non-Jewish people, to mean a code of do's and don'ts. Rather, it should be seen as G-d's instruction and teaching to us so we can understand Him better.

Israel came to Mount Sinai on the third day of the third month (Exodus [*Shemot*] 19:1). The L-rd visited the people three days later (Exodus [*Shemot*] 19:10-17). Therefore, the Torah was given by G-d in the third month of the biblical religious calendar, which is the month of Sivan, on the sixth day of this month. This day is exactly 50 days from the crossing of the Red Sea.

Shavuot (Pentecost) is called the season of the giving of the Torah (*Z'man Matan Toraseinu*) in Hebrew because this is the literal day that G-d revealed Himself to the people of Israel as they stood at the base of Mount Sinai.

2.   **The giving of the Holy Spirit (*Ruach HaKodesh*) by G-d.** *Yeshua* was resurrected on the Feast of First Fruits (*Bikkurim*), as was seen in the previous chapter. Fifty days after the resurrection of *Yeshua*, the Holy Spirit (*Ruach HaKodesh*) came to dwell in the hearts and lives of all the believers in *Yeshua* (Acts 1:8; 2:1-18; Luke 24:49; Joel 2:28-29; Exodus [*Shemot*] 19:16; Isaiah [*Yeshayahu*] 44:3; Deuteronomy [*Devarim*] 16:5-6,16; 2 Kings 21:4).[5]

In the chart below, let's make a comparison between the original Torah covenant given at Mount Sinai with the renewed Torah based covenant in Jeremiah 31:31-33.

Shavuot in the Tanach (Exodus 19)	*Shavuot* in the *Brit Hadashah* (Jeremiah 31:31-33)
—The fiftieth day	—The fiftieth day
—Commandments of G-d written on tablets of stone (Exodus 24:12)	—Commandments of G-d written on our hearts (Jeremiah 31:33; Psalm 40:8; 37:31; Isaiah 51:7; Ezekial 11:19-20 36;26-27; 2 Corinthians 3:3; Hebrews 8:10

—Written by the finger of G-d
  (Exodus 31:18)
—3,000 slain (Exodus 32:1-8,26-28)
—The letter of the Torah

—Mount Sinai (Exodus 19:11)

—Written by the Spirit of G-d
  (2 Corinthians 3:3; Hebrews 8:10)
—3,000 live (Acts 2:38-41)
—The Spirit of the Torah (Romans 2:29;
  7:6; 2 Corinthians 3:6)
—Mount Zion (Romans 11:26; Hebrews
  12:22; 1 Peter 2:6)

Shavuot as a Marriage: A Betrothal Contract

One of the most beautiful images of *Shavuot* (Pentecost) is that of the marriage between G-d (the groom) and Israel (the bride).[6]

In the biblical wedding service that G-d gave (Romans 9:4; Hebrews 9:1; 1 Chronicles 28:11-12), marriage consisted of two stages. The first stage is betrothal, called *erusin* in Hebrew. You enter this first stage of marriage as soon as a betrothal contract (a *shitre erusin*) is made between the two parties. The written contract is called a *ketubah*. During betrothal, you are legally married, but do not physically dwell with your mate. Betrothal is so legally binding that you cannot get out of it without a divorce, called a *get* in Hebrew.

In fact, by understanding the Hebrew language, we can see how betrothal is legally binding. To G-d, Hebrew is the pure language (Zephaniah 3:9), and Hebrew will allow us to understand deeper spiritual truths in the Bible that would be more difficult to understand otherwise. The word for betrothal in Hebrew, *erusin*, comes from the Hebrew verb *aras*. *Aras* is related to the Hebrew word *asar*, which means "to bind."[7] By this, we can see that the Hebrew language communicates to us that betrothal is legally binding.

Messianic Fulfillment. In the New Testament (*Brit Hadashah*), we can see that Joseph (*Yosef*) was betrothed to

Mary (*Miryam*) when the angel Gabriel announced to Mary (*Miryam*) that she would have a son named *Yeshua* (Jesus), by the Holy Spirit (*Ruach HaKodesh*) of G-d, who would be the Messiah (Luke 1:26-35). When Joseph (*Yosef*) discovered that his betrothed (espoused) wife Mary (*Miryam*) was pregnant, he decided to get a divorce (*get*) until the angel of the L-rd changed his mind by appearing to him in a dream (Matthew [*Mattityahu*] 1:18-20).

Betrothal is mentioned in the Torah in Exodus (*Shemot*) 21:8; Leviticus (*Vayikra*) 19:20; Deuteronomy (*Devarim*) 20:7; 22:23. The second stage of marriage is the fullness or consummation of the marriage. This stage of marriage is called *nesu'in*.

The Bible tells us in Jeremiah (*Yermiyahu*) 2:2 that at Mount Sinai, G-d betrothed Himself to Israel, as it is written:

> *Go and cry in the ears of Jerusalem, saying, Thus saith the Lord; I remember thee, the kindness of thy youth, the love of thine espousals, when thou wentest after Me in the wilderness, in a land that was not sown. Israel was holiness unto the Lord, and the first-fruits of His increase...* (Jeremiah [*Yermiyahu*] 2:2-3).

In Exodus 19, when G-d by the leading of Moses (*Moshe*) brought the children of Israel to Mount Sinai, G-d betrothed Himself to Israel. On Mount Sinai, G-d gave the Torah to Israel (Exodus [*Shemot*] 20:1-21). At this time, G-d was making a betrothal contract, a *ketubah*, with Israel. The *ketubah* (or written betrothal contract, which is understood to be the Torah) represents "The book of the covenant" (marriage is a covenant) that Moses (*Moshe*) wrote prior to the revelation at Mount Sinai (Exodus [*Shemot*] 24:4,7). The Book of the Covenant spelled out mutual obligations of G-d and Israel just as the *ketubah* spelled out the obligations between husband and wife.[8] So, G-d made a marriage contract with Israel in Exodus (*Shemot*) 19:3-7.

In Exodus (*Shemot*) 19:8, Israel accepts G-d's marriage proposal. Israel answered in Exodus (*Shemot*) 19:8, "All that the Lord hath spoken we will do" (*Na'aseh V'Nishmah*—we agree to do even before we have listened).[9]

In Exodus (*Shemot*) 19:2, Israel camped before the L-rd. The word *camp* in Hebrew is *chanah* and in this case is singular, while Israel is plural. By this we can see that at that time all Israel had become one. This is also a necessary requirement for marriage (Genesis [*Bereishit*] 2:24; Ephesians 5:31).

The biblical wedding ceremony that G-d gave requires that the marriage be consummated under a wedding canopy known as a *chupah*. In Exodus (*Shemot*) 19:17, Moses (*Moshe*) brought forth the people out of the camp to meet G-d and they stood at the nether part of the mount. The word *nether* in Hebrew actually implies that the people stood underneath the mountain. This imagery gives the understanding that the mountain had become a *chupah* and Israel was standing underneath the mountain or under the *chupah*, the place where the wedding takes place.

Every wedding will have two witnesses. They are called the friends of the bridegroom. One is assigned to the groom and one is assigned to the bride. In Exodus (*Shemot*) 19:17, Moses (*Moshe*) is seen as one of the two witnesses whose job is to escort the bride to meet the groom under the *chupah* (Mount Sinai). In order for the *ketubah*, the written contract between the husband and the wife, to be legal in consummating the marriage, it must be signed by the two witnesses, the friends of the bridegroom. Since we can see that Moses

(*Moshe*) was one of the two witnesses, he had to sign the *Ketubah* (Torah) in order for the full marriage between G-d and Israel to be consummated.

However, when Moses (*Moshe*) returned from being with G-d on Mount Sinai, he did not sign the *Ketubah* (Torah). Instead he broke the two tablets (*ketubah*), which were in his right hand (Exodus [*Shemot*] 32:19), thus not signing the *ketubah* which G-d had made with Israel. Therefore, he did not allow Israel to enter into the full marriage. Moses (*Moshe*) broke the two tablets (*ketubah*) when he saw that Israel was worshiping the golden calf and thus were being unfaithful in their marriage.[10]

Spiritual Understanding (Halacha). What does the wedding mean in terms of the Messiah *Yeshua*, and what is the personal application (*halacha*) to us? Messiah *Yeshua* is the groom and the believers in the Messiah are betrothed to Him. When *Yeshua* came to the earth almost 2,000 years ago, He came so that whosoever would put their trust and confidence (*emunah*) in Him would be wedded to Him forever. This would include both Jews and non-Jews (John [*Yochanan*] 3:16). Because *Yeshua* came as the suffering Messiah, Messiah ben Joseph, during His first coming, He ascended to Heaven to be with G-d the Father until He returns during His second coming to be the King Messiah, Messiah ben David. Today, *Yeshua* does not physically dwell with those who trust in Him. Therefore, the believers in the Messiah *Yeshua* are currently spiritually betrothed to Him. We will enter the full marriage and physically dwell with Him during the Messianic age known as the Millennium. However, before we can physically dwell with the Messiah during the Messianic age on earth, the wedding ceremony when the believers in the Messiah *Yeshua* will be wedded to Him must take place.

In the biblical wedding service that G-d gave, after you are married, you have a honeymoon. The honeymoon lasts a week and is known as the seven days of the *chupah*. Seven days equals a week. In Hebrew, a week means a seven. It can mean seven days or seven years (Daniel 9:24-27; Genesis [*Bereishit*] 29:27). In Joel (*Yoel*) 2:16, we see the marriage of the bride (the believers in *Yeshua*) and the bridegroom (*Yeshua*) where the bridegroom is going forth from the chamber and the bride out of her closet. The word *closet* is the Hebrew word *chupah*, and the *chupah* here refers to Heaven. After the honeymoon in Heaven, *Yeshua* will be returning with His bride to attend the marriage supper (Revelation 19:7-14). Then we will rule and reign with Him physically during the Messianic age known as the Millennium (Revelation 20:4).

The Pouring Out of G-d's Holy Spirit (*Ruach HaKodesh*)

In Exodus (*Shemot*) 19:19, a trumpet (*shofar*) was sounded. The trumpet (*shofar*) that was sounded grew louder and louder. Exodus (*Shemot*) 19:19 says, "...and God answered him with thunder [by a voice, KJV]." Exodus (*Shemot*) 20:18 says, "And all the people perceived the thunder [saw the thunderings, KJV]...."

In the Midrash, which is a rabbinical commentary on the Scriptures, in Exodus Rabbah 5:9, it says:

When G-d gave the Torah on Sinai He displayed untold marvels to Israel with His voice. What happened?

G-d spoke and the voice reverberated throughout the whole world... It says, And all the people witnessed the thunderings [Exodus (*Shemot*) 20:18].

Note that it does not say "the thunder" but "the thunderings"; wherefore, R. Johanan said that G-d's voice, as it was uttered split up into seventy voices, in seventy languages, so that all the nations should understand...

In Deuteronomy 32:8 it is written, "When the Most High divided to the nations their inheritance, when He separated the sons of Adam, He set the bounds of the people according to the number of the children of Israel." In Exodus (*Shemot*) 1:1-5, we can see that the number of the children of Israel who came to Egypt was 70. Therefore, the 70 voices as interpreted by R. Johanan represented all the nations of the world, based upon Deuteronomy (*Devarim*) 32:8 and Exodus (*Shemot*) 1:1-5. So, it was seen that G-d's voice split up into the languages of all the people on the earth to be a witness to them.

In the book *The Midrash Says*, by Rabbi Moshe Weissman, the author wrote:

In the occasion of Matan Torah [the giving of the Torah], the Bnai Yisrael [children of Israel] not only heard Hashem's [the L-rd's] Voice but actually saw the sound waves as they emerged from Hashem's [the L-rd's] mouth. They visualized them as a fiery substance. Each commandment that left Hashem's [the L-rd's] mouth traveled around the entire Camp and then to each Jew individually, asking him, "Do you accept upon yourself this Commandment with all the halochot [Jewish law] pertaining to it?" Every Jew answered "Yes" after each commandment. Finally, the fiery substance which they saw engraved itself on the luchot [tablets].[11]

Messianic Fulfillment. This same experience we just discussed that happened at Mount Sinai also occurred 50 days after the resurrection of *Yeshua* on the day of *Shavuot* (Pentecost) almost 2,000 years ago. This experience is also described in Acts 2:1-11 and Hebrews 12:18-19. In describing what happened in Exodus (*Shemot*) 20:18, Hebrews 12:18-19 says, "And the sound of a trumpet, and the voice of words...." The word *words* in Hebrews 12:19 is the Greek word *rhema*, which means "an individual word." In this passage in Hebrews, we can see the same thing that Rabbi Moshe Weissman understood happened at Mount Sinai in the first *Shavuot* (Pentecost) in his commentary is exactly what did happen as seen in Hebrews 12:19. It is also what happened during the first *Shavuot* (Pentecost) following the resurrection of *Yeshua*. At this *Shavuot* (Pentecost), the people also were as one (Acts 2:1-2; Exodus [*Shemot*] 19:2). When G-d poured out His Holy Spirit (*Ruach HaKodesh*) at this time, once again people began to speak in the different languages of the world (Acts 2:1-11). Therefore, we can see that the *Shavuot* (Pentecost) at Mount Sinai was a rehearsal (*miqra*) of the *Shavuot* (Pentecost) that would occur immediately after the resurrection of *Yeshua*.

The First Trump (*Shofar*) of G-d

Once again in Exodus 19:19, a trumpet (*shofar*) was sounded. This trumpet (*shofar*) grew louder and louder. The Jewish writings understand this to be the first trump (*shofar*) of G-d. The trumpet blown by G-d at Mount Sinai was understood to be the first of the two ram's horns that were present on Mount Moriah during Abraham's (*Avraham*) sacrifice of Isaac (*Yitzchak*) in Genesis 22.

The Jewish people understood that there are three primary trumpets (*shofarim*) that mark major events in the redemptive plan of God. These three trumpets are known as the first trump, the last trump, and the great trumpet. Genesis (*Bereishit*) 22 is one of the most important Torah readings to the Jewish people. In some Jewish circles, it is read every day of the week except for the sabbath. It is also the primary Torah reading for *Rosh HaShanah*. The theme of the chapter includes the binding of Isaac on the altar, known in Hebrew as the *Akeidah*, in addition to the phrase "to be seen." The key verse concerning the phrase "to be seen" is Genesis (*Bereishit*) 22:14, as it is written, "And Abraham called the name of that place Jehovah-jireh [the L-rd will see or provide]: as it is said to this day, In the mount of the Lord it shall be seen." Genesis (*Bereishit*) 22:4 says, "Then on the third day Abraham lifted up his eyes, and saw the place afar off."

Messianic Fulfillment. *Yeshua* referred to this event which happened to Abraham (*Avraham*), in John (*Yochanan*) 8:56, as it is written, "Your father Abraham rejoiced to see My day: and he saw it, and was glad." What did Abraham (*Avraham*) see? What took place on Mount Moriah? Abraham (*Avraham*) was instructed by G-d to take Isaac (*Yitzchak*) to Mount Moriah and sacrifice him there (Genesis [*Bereishit*] 22:2). The first and second temples (*Beit HaMikdash*) were built in Jerusalem (*Yerushalayim*) on Mount

Moriah (2 Chronicles 3:1). It was in Jerusalem (*Yerusha-layim*) on Mount Moriah where *Yeshua* was crucified on the tree. Calvary (Golgotha) was located on Mount Moriah. Abraham (*Avraham*) in Genesis (*Bereishit*) 22:4 was looking into the future and seeing that G-d was going to offer up the Messiah to be slain on Mount Moriah at a future time.

G-d called Abraham (*Avraham*) to sacrifice Isaac (*Yitzchak*) and offer him as a burnt offering, known in Hebrew as an *olah*. This is mentioned in Genesis (*Bereishit*) 22:2-3,6,8,13. A burnt offering (*olah*) is an offering that is totally consumed. It is freely given and done freely, willingly, and joyfully by both parties involved. The Bible tells us that G-d freely offered up *Yeshua* joyfully and *Yeshua* was willing and obedient to His death on the tree (Philippians 2:8). In Isaiah (*Yeshayahu*) 53:10, it says that it pleased G-d to offer up *Yeshua*.

When Abraham (*Avraham*) offered up Isaac (*Yitzchak*), Abraham believed that G-d would raise Isaac (*Yitzchak*) from the dead (Hebrews 11:17-19). Abraham (*Avraham*) went willingly, joyfully, and obediently because he believed G-d would raise Isaac (*Yitzchak*) from the dead. This can be seen in Genesis (*Bereishit*) 22:5. In this, we can see that Abraham was a type and picture of G-d the Father, and Isaac (*Yitzchak*) was a type and picture of *Yeshua* the Messiah. In Genesis (*Bereishit*) 22:8, Abraham (*Avraham*) said to Isaac (*Yitzchak*) that G-d would provide a lamb; *Yeshua* was the lamb that G-d offered to us (John [*Yochanan*] 1:29).

This story is an example of the Hebrew expression, "Here now, but not yet." Abraham (*Avraham*) offered up his only son (Genesis [*Bereishit*] 22:16; Hebrews 11:17), and G-d offered up His only Son, *Yeshua* (John [*Yochanan*] 3:16). Instead of Isaac (*Yitzchak*), Abraham (*Avraham*) offered up a ram as the ram was found caught in the thicket (Genesis [*Bereishit*] 22:13). In the Hebrew writings, the ram represents the Messiah and the thicket stands for the sins of the people. In Genesis (*Bereishit*) 22:13 where it says "behind him," the Hebrew word is *achar*, which means afterward or in the future. Therefore, the imagery presented here is that Abraham (*Avraham*) saw this ram being sacrificed in the future. This is what *Yeshua* was referring to in John (*Yochanan*) 8:56.

Once again, relating to the story in Genesis 22, the left horn of the ram that was caught in the thicket (Genesis [*Bereishit*] 22:13) is called the first trump (*shofar*) and the right horn of the ram is called the last trump (*shofar*).[12]

The Three Trumpets (*Shofarim*) of G-d

The three great trumpets (*shofarim*) that mark major events in the redemptive plan of G-d are associated with days in the biblical calendar. The first trump is associated with and was blown by G-d on the Feast of *Shavuot* (Pentecost) when G-d gave the Torah to the Jewish people at Mount Sinai (Exodus [*Shemot*] 19:19).

The last trump is associated with and is blown on *Rosh HaShanah*. (*Rosh HaShanah* will be discussed in the next chapter.) The biblical name for *Rosh HaShanah* is *Yom Teruah*, which in Hebrew means "the day of the awakening blast." This trump (*shofar*) is mentioned by the apostle Paul

(*Rav Sha'ul*) in First Corinthians 15:51-53. Because the last trump is only blown on *Rosh HaShanah* and because the apostle Paul (*Rav Sha'ul*) specifically mentions that the rapture (*natzal*) of the believers in *Yeshua* the Messiah will take place at the last trump, the apostle Paul (*Rav Sha'ul*) was giving a clear understanding that the rapture of the believers in Messiah will happen on a *Rosh HaShanah*.

The great trump (*shofar HaGadol*) is associated with and is blown on *Yom Kippur*. *Yeshua* said that He would return at His second coming at the sound of the great trump (Matthew [*Mattityahu*] 24:30-31). Because the great trump (*shofar Ha-Gadol*) is only blown on *Yom Kippur* and because *Yeshua* said that He would return with the sound of a great trump, *Yeshua* was stating very clearly that He would return on a *Yom Kippur*. (This will be discussed in more detail in the chapter concerning *Yom Kippur*.) Thus, the first and last trump will relate to the ram's horn in Genesis (*Bereishit*) 22. Again, the first trump (*shofar*) will be the left horn of the ram and the last trump (*shofar*) will be the right horn of the ram. In Exodus (*Shemot*) 19:19, the trumpet (*shofar*) that was blown by G-d will be the first trump.

The Spiritual Understanding of *Shavuot* (Pentecost)

Spiritual Application (Halacha). The giving of the Torah at Mount Sinai involved the Aaronic priesthood, the sacrificial system, the tabernacle, the sabbath days, the festivals, the civil and ceremonial laws, and the Ten Commandments (Exodus [*Shemot*] 19:17,20; 20:1,21-22; 21:1-2,12; 22:1,16; 23:10-11,14; 24:1-8,12,18; 25:1,8-9,40; 28:1; 31:12-18; 32:1; 34:27-28; Hebrews 8:1-6; 9:1-12,15,18-24; 10:1,10;

13:20). These things were given by G-d as a shadow of things to come (Hebrews 10:1) to teach us (Galatians 3:24) about the Messiah *Yeshua* and the redemptive work of G-d (Colossians 2:16-17). *Shavuot* (Pentecost) was the birth of the congregation (*kehilat*) in the wilderness (Acts 7:38). The things given at Mount Sinai were divine and from G-d, but shown in a physical way (Hebrews 9:1) to enable us to understand the spiritual truths that G-d wanted to communicate to us (1 Peter 2:5-9). So G-d gave Israel the covenant, the Torah, the services, the oracles of G-d, and the promises (Romans 9:4-5; 3:2), which were divine (Hebrews 9:1), at Mount Sinai to teach us about the Messiah (Psalm [*Tehillim*] 40:7). With this in mind, let's look at the spiritual understandings that G-d was communicating to us at *Shavuot*.

The Two Leavened Wave Loaves
(Leviticus [*Vayikra*] 23:15-17)

This was to be a new meal offering to the L-rd (Leviticus [*Vayikra*] 23:16; Numbers [*Bamidbar*] 28:26). There were to be two wave loaves baked with leaven (Leviticus [*Vayikra*] 23:17). At Passover (*Pesach*), leaven was absolutely forbidden (Exodus [*Shemot*] 12:15,19-20) and in the regular meal offering, no leaven was permitted (Leviticus [*Vayikra*] 2:1,4-5, 11). We saw earlier that leaven represents sin (1 Corinthians 5:6-8; Galatians 5:9). Passover (*Pesach*) and Unleavened Bread (*Hag HaMatzah*) spoke of the death and burial of *Yeshua* who was without sin. Yet on *Shavuot* (Pentecost), G-d commanded just the opposite. Why?

Shavuot (Pentecost) speaks of the birth of Israel as a nation, as well as the birth of the congregation (*kehilat*) of believers in *Yeshua* through the Holy Spirit (*Ruach HaK-odesh*). The two loaves speak of Israel and the congregation of believers in the Messiah. Even though both Israel and the congregation (*kehilat*) of believers in the Messiah *Yeshua* are chosen by G-d and are holy to Him, sin is still found in Israel and sin still exists in the congregation of believers. Passover (*Pesach*) and Unleavened Bread (*Hag HaMatzah*) speak primarily of *Yeshua* who is without sin, but *Shavuot* (Pentecost) speaks of Israel and the congregation (*kehilat*) of believers where sin still exists.

We have just stated that the two wave loaves speak of Israel and the congregation (*kehilat*) of believers in the Messiah. The number two in the Bible is the number of witness and testimony. For example, two witnesses in the Bible establishes a truth (Matthew [*Mattityahu*] 18:19-20; Deuteronomy [*Devarim*] 19:15; John 5:30-33,36-37; Luke 24:44; 1 John 5:8; Revelation 12:11; 11:3). The Ten Commandments were written on two stones (Exodus [*Shemot*] 31:18). Also, the Ten Commandments are fulfilled by obeying two commandments (Matthew [*Mattityahu*] 22:34-40). Messiah and His congregation (*kehilat*) of believers testify of the love, grace, and plan of G-d for the whole world.

The meal offering was to be an offering burned by fire upon the altar. A work of the Holy Spirit (*Ruach HaKodesh*) is an immersion (baptism) of fire (Luke 3:16). Fire is what G-d uses to burn sin out of the lives of a believer in the Messiah (1 Corinthians 3:13-15; 1 Peter 1:7). The followers of *Yeshua* are supposed to live a righteous (*tzaddik*) life before G-d (Ephesians 4:17-32; 5:1-13; Colossians 3:1-13; Romans 8:1-4).

Two-tenths Ephod of Fine Flour
(Leviticus [*Vayikra*] 23:17)

The grinding and crushing of wheat produces fine flour. The fine flour speaks of the refining process that our faith goes through as we are conformed to the image of Messiah *Yeshua* and enter into His trials, testings, temptations, and sufferings (Zechariah 13:9; Romans 5:3-5; 8:29,35-39; 2 Corinthians 1:3-11; 1 Peter 1:7; 4:12-19; Revelation 3:18).

Messianic Fulfillment. *Yeshua* was the wheat that was planted into the ground (John [*Yochanan*] 12:24; 1 Corinthians 15:35-38,42-44). As wheat is beaten and refined to become fine flour, so the Messiah was beaten and bruised as He became that fine flour (Isaiah [*Yeshayahu*] 28:28; 52:14; 53:1-6; Psalm [*Tehillim*] 81:16; 147:14).

Holy to the L-rd for the Priest
(Leviticus [*Vayikra*] 23:20)

Even though the two wave loaves were leavened, the L-rd counted them holy unto Himself for the priest. As mentioned earlier, the two wave loaves that the priest waved represented both Israel and the congregation (*kehilat*) of believers in *Yeshua*. Both the Jewish believers in *Yeshua*, represented by Israel, and the non-Jewish believers, represented by the congregation (*kehilat*), consist of individuals who are leaven. We still sin before G-d despite being believers in the Messiah. In spite of this sin, because we are believers in *Yeshua* and seek to serve and love Him with all our hearts, we are considered holy before G-d (Deuteronomy [*Devarim*] 7:6-8; 14:2; Luke 1:68,72-75; Ephesians 1:4; 5:27; Colossians 1:22-24; 1 Thessalonians 4:7; Titus 2:12; 1 Peter 1:15-16).

A Statute Forever
(Leviticus 23:21)

The Holy Spirit came to dwell with the believer in *Yeshua* forever (John [*Yochanan*] 14:16-17). Therefore, the followers of *Yeshua* should have a continual *Shavuot* (Pentecost) experience; one on a daily basis.

The Feast of Harvest of First Fruits
(Exodus 23:16; 34:22; Numbers 28:26)

Shavuot (Pentecost) is called the Feast of Weeks, the Feast of Harvest, or the Feast of the First Fruits. Passover (*Pesach*) was the barley harvest and *Shavuot* (Pentecost) was the wheat harvest (Exodus [*Shemot*] 34:22; Ruth 1:22; 2:23; Joel 1:11).

Israel was called a land of barley and wheat (Deuteronomy [*Devarim*] 8:7-8; 2 Chronicles 2:15; Jeremiah [*Yermiyahu*] 41:8). The spring wheat and barley harvest preceded the major harvest in the fall, the Feast of Ingathering (Exodus [*Shemot*] 23:16; 34:22). Both the spring and the fall harvests were dependent upon the rains coming at the right time. The fall rains are called the early rain. The spring rains are called the latter rain. The early rain is spoken of in Deuteronomy (*Devarim*) 11:10-15; 28:12; Leviticus (*Vayikra*) 26:4; Joel 2:23,28-29; and Zechariah 10:1. The rain is prophetic of the outpouring of the Holy Spirit (*Ruach HaKodesh*) upon people's lives individually as they accept *Yeshua* into their lives and allow the Holy Spirit to teach and instruct them concerning the ways of G-d. The early rain and the latter rain also teach us about the pouring out of G-d's Holy Spirit in a corporate way upon all flesh. The early rain refers to the outpouring of the Holy Spirit (*Ruach HaKodesh*) during *Yeshua's* first coming and the latter rain refers to the outpouring of the

Holy Spirit (*Ruach HaKodesh*) during *Yeshua's* second coming.

As we are seeing, the harvest speaks of the salvation of people. The spring harvest was the beginning of the harvest of people who would come to receive Yeshua as Messiah with the greatest harvest being at the end of this age (Matthew [*Mattityahu*] 13:39; 9:37-38; Mark 4:29). The fall harvest or the harvest at the end of this present age (*Olam Hazeh*) is in the seventh month on the biblical religious calendar. *Shavuot* (Pentecost) is in the third month. From *Shavuot* (Pentecost), there are four months until the final harvest in the fall (John [*Yochanan*] 4:34-35). The fall harvest is the fruit harvest.

Messianic Fulfillment. G-d said that the coming of *Yeshua* would be like the former and latter rain on the earth (Hosea 6:1-3; Joel 2:23). James (*Ya'akov*) ties the coming of the L-rd to the early and latter rain (James [*Ya'akov*] 5:7). *Yeshua's* death, burial, and resurrection was in the spring of the year; the outpouring of the Holy Spirit after the resurrection of *Yeshua* was in the spring of the year; and all those who believed were first fruits of the entire harvest and were a part of the spring harvest. *Yeshua's* second coming will be in the fall of the year and the greatest number of believers will believe at this time. *Yeshua* spoke about this great harvest at the end of this present age (*Olam Hazeh*) in Matthew (*Mattityahu*) 13:39; 24:13-14; and Revelation 14:6,15-16.

A Harvest of Freewill Offerings and Rejoicing
(Deuteronomy [*Devarim*] 16:9-11,16-17)

As believers in *Yeshua*, when we come before G-d we are to give of ourselves, including our time, talents, and money, and present them before Him with a joyful heart (Acts 4:32-37; 1 Corinthians 16:1-2; 2 Corinthians 8–9).[13]

The Conclusion of the Spring Festivals

This concludes the study of the spring festivals. We have seen how the spring festivals are applicable in three dimensions. They are historic to the nation of Israel; they are fulfilled in the Messiah *Yeshua*; and they describe how the individual believer is to walk (*halacha*) and live his life before G-d. In other words, we can see that G-d has a plan for every individual to willingly come to Him. So the spring festivals were not only historic, but they were also our type and example (1 Corinthians 10:1-2,6,11).

To natural Israel, Passover (*Pesach*) was their freedom from the bondage of Egypt (*Mitzrayim*) (Exodus [*Shemot*] 12). Unleavened Bread (*Hag HaMatzah*) was the separation from the land of Egypt into the immersion (baptism) into the Red Sea and the Cloud in the wilderness (1 Corinthians 10:1-2). Finally, G-d led the people to Mount Sinai (Exodus [*Shemot*] 19:1) where they experienced *Shavuot* (Pentecost) and G-d revealed Himself to the people in a deeper and greater way than He ever did previously.

Messianic Fulfillment. The spring festivals were fulfilled by *Yeshua*. Messiah, who was our Passover Lamb, died on the day of Passover (*Pesach*). He was without sin and is the Bread of Life. *Yeshua* was in the sepulcher on the day of Unleavened Bread (*Hag HaMatzah*) and He was the kernel of wheat that was buried in the earth. *Yeshua* arose as First Fruits of the barley harvest, He Himself being the first of those to rise from the dead and receive a resurrected body.

Finally, the Holy Spirit (*Ruach HaKodesh*) was poured out upon all flesh during the feast of *Shavuot* (Pentecost) to gather all believers in the Messiah to be G-d's spring harvest in the earth. As these four feasts describe in detail the significant events during the first coming of Messiah when He came as the suffering Messiah, Messiah ben Joseph, to redeem both man and the earth back to G-d following the fall of man in the Garden of Eden, we will find that the fall festivals give us tremendous insight and understanding concerning the events of *Yeshua's* second coming. Then He will return as the King of Kings and Lord of Lords and come back to earth as the kingly Messiah, Messiah ben David, to rule and reign on earth during the Messianic age or the Millennium.

Spiritual Application (Halacha). Every time a person receives *Yeshua* the Messiah as his own Savior, he spiritually experiences Passover (*Pesach*). He is to flee Egypt (the world's evil system and ways) and trust (*emunah*) in the Messiah, the Lamb of God, and allow *Yeshua* to be the doorpost of his heart. As believers, we are then to seek to live holy lives before G-d and experience Unleavened Bread (*Hag HaMatzah*). Just as *Yeshua* arose from the dead, we are to consider our former ways dead to us and experience the newness of life in the Messiah. Once we do this, we can be immersed (baptized) in the Holy Spirit (*Ruach HaKodesh*) and have the power of G-d (the anointing) in our lives. At that time, G-d will begin to take us on a spiritual journey through the wilderness of life.

In the process of experiencing life's bitter disappointments and struggles, if we keep our eyes upon G-d, He will take us from Passover (*Pesach*) to *Shavuot* (Pentecost) where He will reveal His ways and His Word, the Bible, in a deeper and progressive way. By keeping our eyes on the Messiah through life's struggles, G-d will not only reveal His Word, the Bible, to us in a greater way, but He also will refine our faith like fine flour just as was done to the wheat. Meanwhile, if we put our entire trust (*emunah*) in *Yeshua* through our spiritual journey in the wilderness of life as G-d refines our faith and reveals Himself to us in a greater way, our spiritual journey will not end in the wilderness of life. Instead G-d will take us forward to spiritually experience the fall festivals and our spiritual promised land. It is when we spiritually experience the fall festivals, especially the Feast of Tabernacles (*Sukkot*), and enter into our spiritual promised land that G-d will anoint our lives for Him in an awesome way as we live and serve Him. We will then experience the greatest joy in our entire lives. Joy unspeakable! This is what the Feast of Tabernacles (*Sukkot*) is all about. It is called "the season of our joy" and this joy is what we have to look forward to as we read about the fall festivals in the following chapters.

Chapter 7

Rosh HaShanah

The Season of *Teshuvah*

A special season known as *Teshuvah*, which in Hebrew means "to return or repent," begins on the first day of the month of Elul and continues 40 days, ending with *Yom Kippur*. Thirty days into *Teshuvah*, on Tishrei 1, comes *Rosh HaShanah*. This begins a final ten-day period beginning on *Rosh HaShanah* and ending on *Yom Kippur*. These are known as the High Holy Days and as the Awesome Days (*Yamim Nora'im*, the days of awe). The sabbath that falls within this ten-day period is called *Shabbat Shuvah*, the Sabbath of Return. Five days after *Yom Kippur* is *Sukkot*, the Feast of Tabernacles. *Teshuvah* begins on Elul 1 and concludes on Tishrei 10, *Yom Kippur*. Each morning during the 30 days of the month of Elul, the trumpet (*shofar*) or ram's horn is blown to warn the people to repent and return to G-d.[1]

Teshuvah (repentance) speaks to all people. Those who believe in the Messiah are called to examine their lives and see where they have departed from G-d. It is a call to examine the Scriptures and the evidence that the Messiah was who He said He was.

G-d has always had a heart to warn people before He proclaims judgment. G-d warned the people before the flood, and He warned Nineveh before it was ruined. He does not want anyone to receive the wrath of His judgment (Ezekiel [*Yechezekel*] 18:21-23,30-32; Zephaniah 2:1-3; 33:1-7; 2 Peter 3:9).

The whole month of Elul is a 30-day process of preparation through personal examination and repentance for the coming High Holy Days. The *shofar* is blown after every morning service. Psalm 27, which begins with "The Lord is my light and my salvation," is also recited at the end of the morning and evening liturgy.[2] The message from Elul 1 to *Rosh HaShanah* is clear: Repent before *Rosh HaShanah*. Don't wait until after *Rosh HaShanah*, or you will find yourself in the Days of Awe.

There are idioms or phrases that help us identify the days in the season of *Teshuvah* (repentance). Just as unfamiliar foreigners may be confused when they hear Americans call Thanksgiving Day, "Turkey Day" or "Pilgrims' Day," non-Jewish believers in *Yeshua* can be confused by the different terms for the major feasts of the L-rd.[3]

Rosh HaShanah: Names, Themes, and Idioms

1. *Teshuvah* (repentance)
2. *Rosh HaShanah* (Head of the Year, Birthday of the World)
3. *Yom Teruah* (the Day of the Awakening Blast/Feast of Trumpets)
4. *Yom HaDin* (the Day of Judgment)
5. *HaMelech* (the Coronation of the Messiah)

6. *Yom HaZikkaron* (the Day of Remembrance or memorial)
7. The time of Jacob's (*Ya'akov*) trouble (the birthpangs of the Messiah, *Chevlai shel Mashiach*)
8. The opening of the gates
9. *Kiddushin/Nesu'in* (the wedding ceremony)
10. The resurrection of the dead (rapture, *natzal*)
11. The last trump (*shofar*)
12. *Yom Hakeseh* (the hidden day)[4]

Rosh HaShanah: The Head of the Year (Birthday of the World)

Rosh HaShanah marks the Jewish New Year and is a part of the season of repentance. *Rosh* in Hebrew means "chief or head" and *shanah* means "year." *Rosh HaShanah* is the head of the year on the civil calendar, and is also known as the birthday of the world since the world was created on this day (Talmud, Rosh Hashanah 11a).

Jewish tradition believes that Adam was created on this day (Mishnah, San Hedrin 38b). How did they decide that this was the day of the year the world was created? Because the first words of the Book of Genesis (*Bereishit*), "in the beginning," when changed around, read, *Aleph b'Tishrei*, or "on the first of Tishrei." Therefore, *Rosh HaShanah* is known as the birthday of the world, for tradition tells us that the world was created then.[5]

Note: There are four new years in the Jewish calendar. Nisan 1 is the New Year's day of kings (the date for determining how many years a king has ruled) and for months (Nisan is the first month). Elul 1 is the new year for the tithing of animals. Shevat 15 (Tu Bishvat) is the new year for the trees, and Tishrei 1 is the new year of years. It also marks the anniversary of the creation of the world.[6]

Time of Observance

Rosh HaShanah is observed for two days. It comes on the first and second days of the Hebrew month of Tishrei (usually in September or October), which is the first month of the biblical civil calendar.[7] The month of Tishrei is the seventh month in the biblical religious calendar. This may seem strange that *Rosh HaShanah*, the New Year, is on the first and second day of Tishrei, the seventh month on the biblical religious calendar. The reason that *Rosh HaShanah* is the seventh month in the biblical religious calendar is that G-d made the month of Nisan the first month of the year in remembrance of Israel's divine liberation from Egypt (Exodus [*Shemot*] 12:2; 13:4). However, according to tradition, the world was created on Tishrei, or more exactly, Adam and Eve were created on the first day of Tishrei and it is from Tishrei that the annual cycle began. Hence, *Rosh HaShanah* is celebrated at this time.[8]

Why Is *Rosh HaShanah* Two Days Long?

Unlike other festivals that are celebrated in the Diaspora (the dispersion, referring to Jews who live outside of the Holy Land of Israel) *Rosh HaShanah* is celebrated for two days because of uncertainty about observing the festivals on the correct calendar day. *Rosh HaShanah* is the only holiday celebrated for two days in Israel. As with all other festivals, the uncertainty was involved in a calendar that depended on when the new moon was promulgated, designating the beginning of each new month by the rabbinical court in

Jerusalem (*Yerushalayim*) in ancient times. The problem of *Rosh HaShanah* is heightened by the fact that it falls on *Rosh Chodesh*, the new moon itself. Therefore, even in Jerusalem (*Yerushalayim*), it would have been difficult to let everyone know in time that the New Year had begun. To solve this problem, a two-day *Rosh HaShanah* was practiced even in Israel. Creating a two-day *Rosh HaShanah* was also intended to strengthen observance of each day; in the rabbinic view, the two days are regarded as a *yoma arikhta*, one long day.[9]

Yom Teruah: The Day of the Awakening Blast

In Psalm (*Tehillim*) 98:6 it is written, "With trumpets and the sound of the horn shout joyfully before the King, the Lord" (NAS). The blessing we receive from G-d when we understand the meaning of *Rosh HaShanah* and the blowing of the trumpet (*shofar*) is found in Psalm (*Tehillim*) 89:15, as it is written, "How blessed are the people who know the joyful sound [blast of the *shofar*]…" (NAS).

Rosh HaShanah is referred to in the Torah as *Yom Teruah*, the Day of the Sounding of the *Shofar*[10] (or the Day of the Awakening Blast). On *Yom Teruah*, the Day of the Sounding of the *Shofar*, it is imperative for every person to hear (*shema*) the *shofar*.[11] The *mitzvah* (or biblical commandment [John (*Yochanan*) 14:15]) of the *shofar* is to hear (*shema*) the *shofar* being blown, not actually blow it yourself, hence the blessing, "to hear the sound of the *shofar*."[12]

Teruah means "an awakening blast." A theme associated with *Rosh HaShanah* is the theme "to awake." *Teruah* is also translated as "shout." The Book of Isaiah (*Yeshayahu*), chapter 12, puts the shouting in the context of the thousand-year reign of Messiah, the *Athid Lavo*. The Messianic era and shout is mentioned in Isaiah (*Yeshayahu*) 42:11; 44:23; Jeremiah (*Yermiyahu*) 31:7; and Zephaniah 3:14. The first coming of *Yeshua* is associated with a shout in Zechariah 9:9. The ultimate shout is the rapture (*natzal*) in First Thessalonians 4:16-17.[13]

Whether it is by the blast of a *shofar* or the force of a supernatural shout, G-d's goal is to awaken us! For this reason it is written, "...Awake, sleeper, and arise from the dead, and Christ will shine on you" (Ephesians 5:14 NAS). The Book of Ephesians has many references to *Rosh HaShanah* and the High Holy Days. For example, in Ephesians 4:30, being sealed unto the day of redemption refers to *Yom Kippur*, the Day of Atonement. G-d gave this festival to teach us that we will be judged on *Rosh HaShanah* and will be sealed unto the closing of the gates (*neilah*) on *Yom Kippur*.

Isaiah (*Yeshayahu*) 26:19 speaks of the resurrection. The word *awake* is associated with the resurrection, as it is written, "Your dead will live; their corpses will rise. You who lie in the dust, awake and shout for joy, for your dew is as the dew of the dawn, and the earth will give birth to the departed spirits" (Isaiah [*Yeshayahu*] 26:19 NAS).

The theme of awakening from sleep is used throughout the Bible. It is found in John (*Yochanan*) 11:11; Romans 13:11; Daniel 12:1-2; and Psalm (*Tehillim*) 78:65. In Isaiah 51:9 it is written, "Awake, awake, put on strength, O arm of the Lord; awake as in the days of old, the generations of long ago..." (NAS). The arm of the L-rd is used as a term for the Messiah in Isaiah (*Yeshayahu*) 53:1. The word *arm* is the Hebrew word *zeroah*. During Passover (*Pesach*), a shankbone, known as the *zeroah*, is put on the plate. So, "awake" is a term or idiom for *Rosh HaShanah*. In Isaiah (*Yeshayahu*) 51:9 quoted earlier, the awakening is associated with the coming of the Messiah.[14]

The *shofar* is the physical instrument that G-d instructed us to use to hear (*shema*) the sound of the *shofar* teaching us to awake from spiritual slumber (1 Corinthians 15:46).

In the days of old, the *shofar* was used on very solemn occasions. We first find the *shofar* mentioned in connection with the revelation on Mount Sinai, when the voice of the *shofar* was exceedingly strong and all the people who were in the camp trembled (Exodus [*Shemot*] 19:16b). Thus, the *shofar* we hear on *Rosh HaShanah* ought to remind us of our acceptance of the Torah (Bible) and our obligations to it. The *shofar* also used to be sounded when war was waged upon a dangerous enemy. Thus, the *shofar* we hear on *Rosh HaShanah* ought to also serve as a battle cry to wage war against our inner enemy—our evil inclinations and passions as well as the devil, *Ha satan*, himself. The *shofar* was also sounded on the Jubilee Year, heralding freedom from slavery (Leviticus [*Vayikra*] 25:9-10).[15]

Spiritually (*halacha*), this refers to freedom from the slavery of sin, the desires of this world, and serving the devil (Romans 6:12-13; James 4:4).

Another reason for sounding the *shofar* is that *Rosh HaShanah* is the celebration of the birth of creation. G-d began to rule over the world on this day. When a king begins to reign, he is heralded with trumpets. That is why Psalm 47 precedes the blowing of the *shofar*; it is a call to the nations:

"...Sing praises to our King, sing praises. For God is the King of all the earth..." (Psalm [*Tehillim*] 47:6-7 NAS). It also precedes because of the reference to the *shofar* in the previous verse (Psalm 47:5), as it is written "God has ascended with a shout, the Lord, with the sound of a trumpet" (NAS).[16]

In Jewish tradition, many reasons have been offered for the sounding of the *shofar*: The ram's horn is identified with the ram that became the substitute sacrifice for Isaac (*Yitzchak*) in Genesis (*Bereishit*) 22:1-19. The giving of the Torah at Mount Sinai was accompanied by the sounding of the *shofar* (Exodus [*Shemot*] 19:19). The proclamation of the Jubilee was heralded by the blast of the *shofar* (Leviticus [*Vayikra*] 25:9-11); and the commencement of the Messianic age is to be announced by the sound of the great *shofar* (Isaiah [*Yeshayahu*] 27:13). The book *Gates of Repentance* cites Maimonide's call to awaken from spiritual slumber:

> Awake, you sleepers, from your sleep! Rouse yourselves, you slumberers, out of your slumber! Examine your deeds, and turn to G-d in repentance. Remember your Creator, you who are caught up in the daily round, losing sight of eternal truth; you are wasting your years in vain pursuits that neither profit nor save. Look closely at yourselves; improve your ways and your deeds. Abandon your evil ways, your unworthy schemes, every one of you! (Yad Hichot Teshuva 3.4).[17]

When the rabbis saw the phrase, "Awake, O Israel," they would identify those verses with something concerning *Rosh HaShanah*. The blowing of the *shofar* took place at the temple (*Beit HaMikdash*) on *Rosh HaShanah* (Nehemiah 8:1-3).[18]

The *shofar* was also blown at the temple to begin the sabbath each week. There are two types of trumpets used in the Bible:

1. The silver trumpet, and
2. The *shofar*, or ram's horn.

On the sabbath, there was within the temple (*Beit HaMikdash*) a sign on the wall that said, "To the house of the blowing of the trumpet [*shofar*]." Each sabbath (*shabbat*), two men with silver trumpets and a man with a *shofar* made three trumpet blasts twice during the day. On *Rosh HaShanah*, it is different. The *shofar* is the primary trumpet. On *Rosh HaShanah*, a *shofar* delivers the first blast, a silver trumpet the second, and then a *shofar* the third. The silver trumpets and the gathering at the temple are specified in the Book of Numbers (*Bamidbar*) chapter 10.[19]

According to Leviticus (*Vayikra*) 23:24 and Numbers (*Bamidbar*) 29:1, *Rosh HaShanah* is the day of the blowing of the trumpets. According to the Mishnah (Rosh HaShanah 16a; Rosh Hashanah 3:3), the trumpet used for this purpose is the ram's horn, not trumpets made of metal as in Numbers (*Bamidbar*) 10.[20]

The Use of the *Shofar* in the Bible

The *shofar* or ram's horn, has always held a prominent role in the history of G-d's people in the Bible:

1. The Torah was given to Israel with the sound of the *shofar* (Exodus [*Shemot*] 19:19).

2. Israel conquered in the battle of Jericho with the blast of the *shofar* (Joshua 6:20).

3. Israel will be advised of the advent of the Messiah with the sound of the *shofar* (Zechariah 9:14,16).

4. The *shofar* will be blown at the time of the ingathering of the exiles of Israel to their place (Isaiah [*Yeshayahu*] 27:13).

5. The *shofar* was blown to signal the assembly of the Israelites during war (Judges [*Shoftim*] 3:27; 2 Samuel 20:1).

6. The watchman who stood upon Jerusalem's walls blew the *shofar* (Ezekiel [*Yechezekel*] 33:3-6).

7. The *shofar* was blown at the start of the Jubilee year (Leviticus [*Vayikra*] 25:9).

8. The *shofar* is a reminder that G-d is sovereign (Psalm [*Tehillim*] 47:5).

9. The ram's horn, the *shofar*, is a reminder of Abraham's sacrifice of Isaac and God's provision of a ram as a substitute (Genesis [*Bereishit*] 22:13).

10. The *shofar* was blown to announce the beginning of festivals (Numbers [*Bamidbar*] 10:10). The *shofar* was blown to celebrate the new moon on *Rosh Ha-Shanah* (Psalm 81:1-3).

11. The blowing of the *shofar* is a signal for the call to repentance (Isaiah [*Yeshayahu*] 58:1).

12. The blowing of the *shofar* ushers in the day of the L-rd (Joel 2:1).

13. The blowing of the *shofar* is sounded at the rapture of the believers and the resurrection of the dead (1 Thessalonians 4:16).

14. John was taken up to Heaven in the Book of Revelation by the sound of the *shofar* (Revelation 4:1).

15. Seven *shofarim* are sounded when G-d judges the earth during the tribulation (Revelation 8–9).

16. The *shofar* was used for the coronation of kings (1 Kings [*Melachim*] 1:34,39).[21]

Yom HaDin: The Day of Judgment

Another name for *Rosh HaShanah* is *Yom HaDin*, the Day of Judgment. It was seen that on this day, G-d would sit in court and all men would pass before Him to be judged. Three great books will be opened as each man is weighed in the balance and placed into one of three categories (Talmud, Rosh HaShanah 6b). It has been taught that the school of Shammai says that there will be three classes on the final Day of Judgment, one of the wholly righteous, one of the wholly wicked, and one of the intermediates. The wholly righteous are at once inscribed and sealed for life in the world to come; the wholly wicked are at once inscribed and sealed for perdition (Talmud, Rosh HaShanah 16b-17a).

The righteous will be protected during the tribulation period. The wicked will face the wrath of G-d during the tribulation period (*Yamim Nora'im*), known in Hebrew as the *Chevlai shel Mashiach*, and will never repent. The average person has until *Yom Kippur* till his fate is sealed forever. In other words, the average person will have until the end of the seven-year tribulation to repent and turn to G-d. The average person on *Rosh HaShanah* is judged by G-d and is neither written in the book of life or the book of the wicked. His fate is yet to be decided. The average person and the wicked have to go through the "Awesome Days," the tribulation, until they reach *Yom Kippur* (the end of the tribulation when their fate is sealed forever). Once you are written in the book of the wicked, you can never get out of it (Revelation 17:8). These are people who never, ever, will accept the Messiah *Yeshua.*[22]

There are 12 months in the year and there are 12 tribes in Israel. Every month of the Jewish year has its representative tribe. The month of Tishrei is the month of the tribe of Dan. This is of symbolic significance, for when Dan was born to Bilhah, Rachel's maid, Rachel said, "God hath judged me [*dannani*], and hath also heard my voice..." (Genesis [*Bereishit*] 30:6). Dan and din (as in *Yom HaDin*, Day of Judgment) are both derived from the same root, symbolizing that Tishrei is the time of divine judgment and forgiveness. Similarly, every month of the Jewish calendar has its sign of the Zodiac (in Hebrew, *Mazal*). The sign of the Zodiac for Tishrei is Scales. This is symbolic of the Day of Judgment.[23]

HaMelech: The Coronation of the King

The recognition of G-d as King is vividly pictured in the Jewish view of Adam's understanding of his Divine Creator being King over all the Universe. It was late on the sixth day since G-d began the Creation of the world, when Adam opened his eyes and saw the beautiful world around him, and he knew at once that G-d created the world, and him too.

Adam's first words were: "The L-rd is King forever and ever!" and the echo of his voice rang throughout the world. "Now the whole world will know that I am King," G-d said, and He was very pleased. This is the first *Rosh HaShanah*! The first New Year. It was the birthday of Man, and the Coronation Day of the King of Kings![24]

Messianic Understanding

A theme and term associated with *Rosh HaShanah* in Hebrew is *HaMelech* (the King). It was mentioned earlier in this chapter that the *shofar* blown on *Rosh HaShanah* is known as the last trump, which *Rav Sha'ul* (the apostle Paul) mentioned in First Thessalonians 4:16-17. At this time, the believers in the Messiah who are righteous (*tzaddikim*) according to *Yom HaDin* (the Day of Judgment) will be taken to Heaven in the rapture (*natzal*) along with the righteous who had died before this time. On *Rosh HaShanah* the coronation of the Messiah *Yeshua* as King will happen in Heaven (Revelation 5). *Yeshua*, who had come to earth during His first coming to play the role of the suffering Messiah, Messiah ben Joseph (*Yosef*), will be crowned as King over all the earth in preparation for His coming back to earth to reign as King Messiah (Messiah ben David) during the Messianic age, the Millennium, or in Hebrew eschatology, the *Athid Lavo* (Revelation 19:16; 20:4).

Daniel 7:9-14 speaks of this in the Tanach:

I beheld till the thrones were cast down, and the Ancient of days did sit...the judgment was set, and the books were opened. [This is *Rosh HaShanah*, *Yom HaDin*, the Day of Judgment. The books are the book of the righteous, the book of the wicked, and the book of remembrance] … *I saw…one like the Son of man* [this is understood to be the Messiah *Yeshua* (Matthew 24:30; 26:64)] *came with the clouds of heaven* [the clouds are the believers in the Messiah (Hebrews 12:1; Revelation 1:7)]…*And there was given Him dominion, and glory, and a kingdom, that all people, nations, and languages, should serve Him: His dominion is an everlasting dominion, which shall not pass away, and His kingdom that which shall not be destroyed* (Daniel 7:9-10,13-14).

John (*Yochanan*) saw this same thing in the Book of Revelation.

After this I looked, and, behold, a door was opened in heaven [the gates of Heaven are opened on *Rosh Ha-Shanah*, according to Isaiah (*Yeshayahu*) 26:2 and Psalm (*Tehillim*) 118:19-20]: *and the first voice which I heard was as it were of a trumpet* [*Rosh HaShanah* is known as the last trump] *talking with me* [*Rosh Ha-Shanah* is known as *Yom Teruah*, the Day of the Awakening Blast or loud shout (1 Thessalonians 4:16-17)]…*And immediately I was in the spirit: and, behold, a throne was set in heaven, and one sat on the throne* [this is *HaMelech*, the coronation of the Messiah; the coronation ceremony is described in Revelation 5] (Revelation 4:1-2).

The description given here in Revelation matches the account in Daniel 7:9-14.

The Enthronement Ceremony of a King

There are four parts to the enthronement of a Jewish king.

1. **The giving of the decree.** Associated with this is a declaration. This can be seen in Psalm (*Tehillim*) 2:6-7, as it is written, "Yet have I set my king upon My holy hill of Zion. I will declare the decree...." Next, a rod/scepter is given, which is an emblem of a king. Scriptures that refer to the scepter include Genesis (*Bereishit*) 49:10; Numbers (*Bamidbar*) 24:17; Esther 4:11; 5:2; 8:4; Psalm 45:6; and Hebrews 1:8. Scriptures that refer to a rod are in Psalm (*Tehillim*) 2:9; Isaiah (*Yeshayahu*) 11:1,4; and Revelation 2:27; 12:5; 19:16. The scepter is an emblem of a king or royal office and a rod refers to the king ruling and reigning righteously in all matters (Isaiah 11:1,4-5). *Yeshua* is the King Messiah (Isaiah 11:1,4-5; Jeremiah 23:5-6; Zechariah 9:9; Luke 1:32-33; John [*Yochanan*] 1:47-49).

2. **The ceremony of the taking of the throne** (Revelation 5). The king sits on the throne and is anointed as king. The word *Christ* in English comes from the Greek word *Christos* and in Hebrew is *Mashiach*, meaning "the anointed one." *Yeshua* came as a prophet during His first coming (Deuteronomy [*Devarim*] 18:15), was resurrected as the priest (John [*Yochanan*] 20:9,17), and is coming back to earth again as King. Kings in Israel were anointed (2 Samuel 5:3-4; 1 Kings [*Melachim*] 1:39-40, 45-46; 2 Kings 9:1-6).

3. **The acclamation.** During the acclamation, all the people shout, "Long live the king!" (1 Kings [*Melachim*] 1:28-31) Next, all the people clap (Psalm [*Tehillim*] 47:1-2). Psalm 47 is a coronation psalm. Psalm 47:5 is the shout and trumpet of *Rosh HaShanah*. Verse 6 is the

shouting and praising of the king. Verse 8 is the cere-mony of the throne. In verse 9, the believers in the Mes-siah *Yeshua* are gathered in His presence.

4. **Each of the subjects coming to visit the king after he has taken the throne.** In this, they will acknowledge their allegiance to him and receive their commissioning from him as to what their job will be in the kingdom (Isaiah [*Yeshayahu*] 66:22-23; Zechariah 14:16-17; Matthew [*Mattityahu*] 2:2).[25]

Yom HaZikkaron: The Day of Remembrance

Rosh HaShanah is known as *Yom HaZikkaron*, the Day of Remembrance. Leviticus (*Vayikra*) 23:24 calls the day "a memorial" (*zikkaron*). Remembrance is a major theme in the Bible. We can see by examining the following Scriptures that G-d remembers us and that we are to remember G-d in all of our ways.

There are two elements of remembrance:

1. **G-d remembers us** (Genesis [*Bereishit*] 8:1; 9:1,15-16; 19:29; 30:22; Exodus [*Shemot*] 2:24-25; 3:1; 6:2,5; 32:1-3,7,11,13-14; Leviticus [*Vayikra*] 26:14,31-33,38-45; Numbers [*Bamidbar*] 10:1-2,9; Psalm [*Tehillim*] 105:7-8, 42:2-3; 112:6). In fact, G-d has a book of remembrance (Malachi 3:16-18; Exodus [*Shemot*] 32:32-33; Revela-tion 3:5; 20:11-15; 21:1,27).

2. **We must remember G-d** (Exodus [*Shemot*] 13:3; 20:8; Deuteronomy [*Devarim*] 7:17-19; 8:18; 16:3; Numbers [*Bamidbar*] 15:37-41).

In Daniel 7:9-10 it is written:

I kept looking until thrones were set up, and the Ancient of Days took His seat; His vesture was like white snow, and the hair of His head like pure wool. His throne was ablaze with flames, its wheels were a burning fire. A river of fire was flowing and coming out from before Him; thousands upon thousands were attending Him, and myriads upon myriads were standing before Him; the court sat, and the books were opened (Daniel 7:9-10 NAS).

Since the court was seated and the books were opened, it is understood to be *Rosh HaShanah*. The books are the book of the righteous, the book of the wicked, and the book of remembrance. The third book that will be opened is the book of remembrance (*zikkaron*). This is why the common greeting during *Rosh HaShanah* is, "May you be inscribed in the Book of Life."[26]

Spiritual Application (Halacha). In Romans 14:10 it is written, "But you, why do you judge your brother? Or you again, why do you regard your brother with contempt? For we shall all stand before the judgment seat of God [Christ]" (NAS). In Second Corinthians 5:10 it is written, "For we must all appear before the judgment seat of Christ, that each one may be recompensed for his deeds in the body, according to what he has done, whether good or bad" (NAS). This is also discussed in First Corinthians 3:9-15. The works of the believers in Messiah will be judged by G-d, but *not* their salvation. This is a judgment of the believers in *Yeshua* only. All people in this judgment are the believers in

Yeshua only. All people in this judgment will be saved. This is not a judgment of your salvation, but a judgment of your rewards based upon your works. On this day, G-d will open the Book of Life and hold a trial (Talmud, Rosh HaShanah 16b). This is known as the *Bema* judgment.[27]

The Time of Jacob's Trouble: The Birthpangs of the Messiah

The English phrase, *birthpangs of the Messiah*, or the Hebrew *Chevlai shel Mashiach*, is a major theme of the Bible. It is commonly known as the seven-year tribulation period. In Matthew (*Mattityahu*) 24, *Yeshua* describes the signs of the end. "And as He was sitting on the Mount of Olives, the disciples came to Him privately, saying, 'Tell us, when will these things be, and what will be the sign of Your coming, and of the end of the age [*olam Hazeh*]?' " (Matthew 24:3 NAS) *Yeshua* said that these days are the beginning of sorrows (Matthew [*Mattityahu*] 24:8). The Greek word translated as sorrows here is *odin*. This word means "birthpangs." The birthpangs of the Messiah are also spoken of in Jeremiah (*Yermiyahu*) 30:4-7, as it is written:

> *Now these are the words which the Lord spoke concerning Israel and concerning Judah, "For thus says the Lord, 'I have heard a sound of terror, of dread, and there is no peace. Ask now, and see, if a male can give birth* [travail with child?]. *Why do I see every man with his hands on his loins, as a woman in childbirth* [*odin*]? *And why have all faces turned pale? Alas! for that day is great, there is none like it; and it is the time of Jacob's distress* [trouble], *but he will be saved from it'* " (Jeremiah [*Yermiyahu*] 30:4-7 NAS).

The birthpangs are also mentioned in First Thessalonians 5:1-3:

Now as to the times and the epochs [seasons], breth-ren, you have no need of anything to be written to you. For you yourselves know full well that the day of the Lord will come just like a thief in the night. While they are saying, "Peace and safety!" then destruction will come upon them suddenly like birth pangs [odin] upon a woman with child; and they shall not escape (1 Thessalonians 5:1-3 NAS).

It can also be seen in Revelation 12:1-2, as it is written:

And a great sign appeared in heaven: a woman clothed with the sun, and the moon under her feet, and on her head a crown of twelve stars [this is Israel (Genesis [Bereishit] 37:9)]; and she was with child; and she cried out, being in labor [odin] and in pain to give birth (Revelation 12:1-2 NAS).

The Scriptures reveal two synonyms:

1. The birthpangs = the time of Jacob's (*Ya'akov's*) trouble.
2. The time of Jacob's (*Ya'akov's*) trouble = the seven-year tribulation.

This period of time will be Israel's most trying time ever. This period of time is known as the tribulation. Jacob (*Ya'akov*) is Israel. There shall be great tribulation in Israel such as never was since there was a nation (Daniel 12:1). It will also be a time when G-d will ultimately judge sin and all the nations on the earth. Through it, the nation of Israel will be physically saved from total destruction by G-d, and will, as a nation, accept *Yeshua* as the Messiah. "...But he shall be saved out of it" (Jeremiah [*Yermiyahu*] 30:7). In Hosea (*Hoshea*) 5:15 it is written, "I will go and return to My place, till they acknowledge their offence, and seek My face: in their affliction [the *Chevlai shel Mashiach*/tribulation] they will seek Me early."

Israel will face genuine crisis during the time of Jacob's (*Ya'akov's*) trouble. The prophet Zechariah prophesied that two of every three inhabitants of Israel will perish during this time, with a remnant of only one third of the population being saved (Zechariah 13:8-9). In Isaiah (*Yeshayahu*) 13:6-8 it is written:

> *Wail, for the day of the Lord is near! It will come as destruction from the Almighty. Therefore all hands will fall limp, and every man's heart will melt* [see Luke 21:26]. *And they will be terrified, pains and anguish will take hold of them, they will writhe like a woman in labor, they will look at one another in astonishment, their faces aflame* (Isaiah [*Yeshayahu*] 13:6-8 NAS).

Isaiah (*Yeshayahu*) 13:10 corresponds to Matthew (*Mattityahu*) 24:29; Mark 13:24; and Revelation 6:12. Other passages that speak of the birthpangs include Genesis (*Bereishit*) 3:16; 35:16-20; 38:27-28; Isaiah (*Yeshayahu*) 26:16-21; 54:1; 66:7-9; Jeremiah 4:31; 6:24; 13:21; 22:23; Micah (*Michah*) 4:9-10; and John (*Yochanan*) 16:21-22.

There are several stages to Israel's birthing the Messiah.

1. **Isaiah 66:7 is a birth *before* travail.** "*Before* she [Israel] travailed [received the Messiah (*Mashiach*)], she brought forth; before her pain came, she was delivered of

a man child" (Isaiah [*Yeshayahu*] 66:7). Isaiah 66:7 is a birth *before* travail. This happened during the first coming of *Yeshua*, the Messiah. The birthpangs that Israel experienced during *Yeshua's* first coming came after *Yeshua's* death with the destruction of the temple and the dispersion of the Jewish people out of Israel by the Romans in 70 C.E. (Common Era).

2. **Isaiah 66:8 is a birth *after* travail.** Isaiah 66:8 says, "...*as soon as* Zion travailed, she brought forth her children." This will happen before *Yeshua* returns to earth to set foot on the Mount of Olives (Zechariah 14:4) as Israel experiences the hardest time she has ever experienced since she was a nation (Daniel 12:1) in the period of time known as the birthpangs of the Messiah, the *Yamim Nora'im*, or the tribulation. The tribulation and the birthpangs of the Messiah are one and the same thing. What we are seeing in these days is the woman (Israel) becoming larger and larger, coming closer and closer to the time when she is about to give birth.[28]

The Opening of the Gates

The gates of Heaven are opened on *Rosh HaShanah* so the righteous nation may enter (Isaiah [*Yeshayahu*] 26:2; Psalm [*Tehillim*] 118:19-20). Because the gates of Heaven are understood to be open on *Rosh HaShanah*,[29] this is further evidence that the rapture (*natzal*) of the believers in the Messiah *Yeshua* will take place on *Rosh HaShanah*.

Rosh Hashanah: The Wedding of the Messiah

The Bible is a marriage covenant. Both the Tanach (Old Testament) and the *Brit Hadashah* (New Testament) describe how G-d through the *Mashiach* (Messiah), the Bridegroom, is in the process of marrying His bride, the believers in Him who will ultimately live and dwell with Him forever.

G-d ordained and established marriage and its divine sanctity in the Torah, the very first book of the Bible, Genesis (*Bereishit*), when He brought Adam and Eve together to become one flesh (Genesis 2:21-24). In doing so, we have a vivid foreshadowing of the Messiah being married to those who would believe upon Him. Let's examine this closer.

Adam is a type of the Messiah *Yeshua*. Adam was made after the likeness of *Yeshua* (Romans 5:14). *Yeshua* (Jesus) was made in the likeness of Adam (Philippians 2:8). In fact, *Yeshua* is called the last Adam (1 Corinthians 15:45-47). In Genesis 2:21, G-d had a deep sleep fall upon Adam. Sleep is synonymous with death (Daniel 12:2; John [*Yochanan*] 11:11-14; 1 Corinthians 15:51-54; Ephesians 5:14). The deep sleep that G-d caused to fall upon Adam is a picture of the crucifixion and death of *Yeshua*, as Messiah ben Joseph. G-d brought a deep sleep upon Adam so He could take a rib from the side of his flesh. This required the shedding of blood. This is a picture of *Yeshua* who was pierced in the side of His flesh, shedding His own blood when He hung on the tree (John [*Yochanan*] 19:34).

From the rib of Adam, G-d made Eve. Likewise, by the death of *Yeshua* and faith (*emunah*) in Him, G-d established the assembly of believers known in Hebrew as the *kehilat*. The believers in the Messiah, His bride, become wedded to Him by faith (*emunah*). This marriage can be seen in the Tanach (Old Testament) as well as in Jeremiah 23:5-6, as it is written, "...this is His name whereby *He* shall be called,

THE LORD OUR RIGHTEOUSNESS" (Jeremiah [*Yermiyahu*] 23:6). In Jeremiah 33:15-16, it is written, "…this is the name wherewith *she* shall be called, THE LORD OUR RIGHTEOUSNESS" (Jeremiah [*Yermiyahu*] 33:16). So from these passages in Jeremiah, we can see that a wedding is taking place. Therefore, by accepting, trusting, and believing in the Messiah, the bride of Messiah, His followers, become one with Him. These people would include both Jew and non-Jews who have lived since Adam and would include Noah, Abraham, Isaac, Jacob, Moses, David, and Solomon as well as the prophets.

G-d gave the wedding customs, service, and ceremonies to the Jewish people (Romans 3:2; 9:4) to teach us about the Messiah *Yeshua* (Colossians 2:16-17). With this in mind, let's examine the biblical wedding ceremony that G-d gave to the Jewish people. The ancient Jewish wedding ceremony G-d gave to the Jewish people to teach us about the wedding of the Messiah consisted of 12 steps.

1. The selection of the bride.

The bride was usually chosen by the father of the bridegroom. The father would send his trusted servant, known as the agent of the father, to search out the bride. An excellent example of this can be seen in Genesis 24. In this chapter, Abraham (a type of G-d the Father) wishes to secure a bride for Isaac (a type of Messiah) and sends his servant Eliezer (a type of the Holy Spirit [*Ruach HaKodesh*]) to do this task (Genesis [*Bereishit*] 24:2-4; 15:2). It is the role of the Holy Spirit (*Ruach HaKodesh*) to convict the world of sin and lead them to G-d (John [*Yochanan*] 16:7-8). Just as the bride was usually chosen by the father of the bridegroom, so the believers in the Messiah are chosen by G-d (John [*Yochanan*] 15:16). The bridegroom chose the bride and lavished his love upon her and she returned his love. This can be seen in Ephesians 5:25, as it is written, "Husbands, love your wives, even as Christ also loved the church, and gave Himself for it." In Genesis (*Bereishit*) 24, Rebekah (*Rivkah*) consented to marry Isaac (*Yitzchak*) even before she ever met him. Today, the believers in the Messiah *Yeshua* consent to become the bride of Messiah even though we have never seen Him. First Peter (*Kefa*) 1:8 speaks of this, as it is written, "Whom having not seen, ye love; in whom, though now ye see Him not, yet believing, ye rejoice with joy unspeakable and full of glory."

2.   A bride price was established.

A price would have to be paid for the bride. The agreed upon price was called a *mohar* in Hebrew. *Yeshua*, being our bridegroom, paid a very high price for His bride, the body of believers. The price He paid was His life. *Yeshua* considered the price He had to pay for His bride before His death as He went into the Garden of Gethsemane to pray in Matthew (*Mattityahu*) 26:39, as it is written, "And He went a little farther, and fell on His face, and prayed, saying, O My Father, if it be possible, let this cup pass from Me: nevertheless not as I will, but as Thou wilt." *Yeshua* was, in essence, saying, "Father, You have chosen this bride and I have agreed to the terms, but do you realize the price that is being asked for her?" Our *mohar*, our bride price, was His life. First Peter (*Kefa*) 1:18-19 says, "Forasmuch as ye know that ye were not redeemed with corruptible things, as silver and gold, from your vain conversation received by tradition from your fathers; but with the precious blood of Christ, as of a lamb without blemish and without spot." In First Corinthians 6:20 it is written, "For ye are bought with a price: therefore glorify God in your body, and in your spirit, which are God's."

3.   The bride and groom are betrothed to each other.

This is the first stage of marriage known as *kiddushin*. I have spoken at length of betrothal in Chapter 6, concerning *Shavuot*. Remember, betrothal is the first of two steps in the marriage process. Betrothal in Hebrew is known as *erusin* or *kiddushin*. Betrothal legally binds the bride and the groom together in a marriage contract, except they do not physically live together. Historically, G-d betrothed Himself to Israel at Mount Sinai (Jeremiah 2:2; Hosea 2:19-20). Whenever you accept the Messiah into your heart and life, you become betrothed to Him while living on the earth.

4.   A written document is drawn up, known as a *ketubah*. This betrothal contract is called, in Hebrew, a *shitre erusin*.

The *ketubah* is the marriage contract that states the bride price, the promises of the groom, and the rights of the bride. The word *ketubah* means "that which is written." The groom promised to work for her, to honor, support, and maintain her in truth, to provide food, clothing, and necessities, and to live together with her as husband and wife. The *ketubah* was the unalienable right of the bride. The *ketubah* must be executed and signed prior to the wedding ceremony. The Bible is the believer's *ketubah*. All the promises that G-d provided for the believers in the Messiah are legally ours, as it is written in Second Corinthians 1:20, "For all the promises of God in Him are yea, and in Him Amen...."

5. The bride must give her consent.

As we saw in Chapter 6, which dealt with *Shavuot* (Pentecost), G-d betrothed Himself to Israel at Mount Sinai as stated in Jeremiah 2:2. Israel consented to the marriage proposal from G-d and said, "I do," as it is written in Exodus (*Shemot*) 24:3. Likewise, the personal application (*halacha*) to those who desire the Messiah to come into their hearts and lives is to accept His invitation to do so by faith (*emunah*), as it is written in Romans 10:8-10:

> *What, then, does it say? The Word is near you in your mouth and in your heart: that is the word about trust [emunah] which we proclaim, namely, that if you acknowledge publicly with your mouth that Yeshua is Lord and trust in your heart that God raised him from the dead, you will be delivered. For with the heart one goes on trusting and thus continues toward righteousness, while with the mouth one keeps on making public acknowledgments and thus continues toward deliverance* (Romans 10:8-10 Jewish New Testament Version).

So, even today, to become the bride of Messiah you must still say "I do" to Him.

6. Gifts were given to the bride and a cup called the cup of the covenant was shared between the bride and the groom.

The rite of betrothal (*erusin*) is completed when the groom gives something of value to the bride and she accepts it. The gift most often given today is the ring. When the groom places the ring on the bride's finger, the rite of betrothal is completed. This completed rite is known in Hebrew as *kiddushin*, which means "sanctification."

The gifts to the bride are symbols of love, commitment, and loyalty. The gift G-d gives to those who accept the Messiah is the Holy Spirit (*Ruach HaKodesh*) (John [*Yochanan*] 14:26; 15:26-27; Acts 2:38; 2 Corinthians 1:21-22). When *Yeshua* ascended to Heaven, He gave gifts to men (Ephesians 4:7-8). These gifts included righteousness (Romans 5:17-18), eternal life (Romans 6:23), grace (Romans 5:12,14-15), faith (Ephesians 2:8-9), and other spiritual gifts (1 Corinthians 12:1,4). These included wisdom, knowledge, healing, the working of miracles, prophecy, the discerning of spirits, tongues, and interpretation of tongues (1 Corinthians 12:8-11), as well as the gifts of helps and administration (1 Corinthians 12:28).

In addition, at this time the cup of the covenant was shared and sealed between the bride and the groom with the drinking of wine. In doing so, the couple drinks from a common cup. The cup is first given to the groom to sip, and then is given to the bride. This cup, known as the cup of the covenant, is spoken of in Jeremiah 31:31-33, as it is written:

Behold, the days come, saith the Lord, that I will make a new covenant with the house of Israel and with the house of Judah: not according to the covenant that I made with their fathers in the day that I took them by the hand to bring them out of the land of Egypt; which My covenant they brake, although I was an husband unto them, saith the Lord: but this shall be the covenant that I will make with the house of Israel; After those days, saith the Lord, I will put My law in their inward parts, and write it in their hearts; and will be their God, and they shall be My people (Jeremiah [*Yermiyahu*] 31:31-33).

Yeshua spoke of the cup of the New Covenant (*Brit Hadashah*) in Luke 22:20.

7. The bride had a *mikvah* (water immersion), which is a ritual of cleansing.

Mikvah is a Hebrew word that means "pool" or "body of water." *Mikvah* is a ceremonial act of purification by the immersion in water. It indicates a separation from a former way to a new way. In the case of marriage, it indicates leaving an old life for a new life with your spouse (Genesis [*Bereishit*] 2:23-24; Ephesians 5:31). Immersing in the *mikvah* is considered spiritual rebirth. The reason is that a *mikvah* has the power to change a person completely. Concerning the marriage to Israel at Mount Sinai, G-d said in Ezekiel 16:8-9, as it is written, "...I sware unto thee, and entered into a covenant with thee...and thou becamest Mine. Then washed I thee with water...." The washing, or immersion, here refers to that of Israel before the people received the Torah when G-d betrothed Himself to Israel at Mount Sinai (Exodus [*Shemot*] 19:14-15). *Yeshua* spoke to the Pharisee, Nicodemus (*Nakdimon*), that he must be born anew (immersed) to enter into the Kingdom of G-d (John [*Yochanan*] 3:1-7). The believers in the Messiah are to be immersed in the name of *Yeshua* (Acts 19:4). The Holy Spirit (*Ruach HaKodesh*) is the immerser of G-d (Luke 3:16; Acts 1:5; 11:15-16).

8. **The bridegroom departed, going back to his father's house to prepare the bridal chamber.**

At this point, the bridegroom leaves for his father's house to prepare the bridal chamber for his bride. It was understood to be the man's duty to go away to be with his father, build a house, and prepare for the eventual wedding. Before he goes, though, he will make a statement to the bride. "I go to prepare a place for you; if I go, I will return again unto you." This is the same statement *Yeshua* made in John (*Yochanan*) 14:1-3 before He went to His father's house in Heaven, as it is written:

> *Let not your heart be troubled: ye believe in God, believe also in Me. In My Father's house are many mansions: if it were not so, I would have told you. I go to prepare a place for you. And if I go and prepare a place for you, I will come again, and receive you unto Myself; that where I am, there ye may be also* (John [*Yochanan*] 14:1-3).

9. **The bride was consecrated and set apart for a period of time while the bridegroom was away building the house.**

Before the bridegroom could go and get the bride, the groom's father had to be satisfied that every preparation had been made by the son. Only then could he give permission to the son to go and get the bride. In other words, while the bridegroom was working on the bridal chamber, it was the father who "okayed" the final bridal chamber. The bridegroom did not know when his father would declare the bridal chamber fit and send him to go get his bride. This is exactly what *Yeshua* was referring to in Mark 13:32-37.

Meanwhile, the bride was to wait eagerly for the return of the bridegroom. In the mind of the bride, the bridegroom could come at any time, even in the middle of the night or at midnight. Therefore, she had to be ready at all times. *Yeshua* referred to this in Mark 13:32-37 and Matthew 25:1-13. While waiting for her bridegroom to come, the bride had to have thought to herself, "Is he really coming back for me? Is he really going to keep his word?" This was the thought that Peter (*Kefa*) answered in Second Peter 3:1-13.

10. **The bridegroom would return with a shout, "Behold, the bridegroom comes" and the sound of the ram's horn (*shofar*) would be blown.**

The time of the return of the bridegroom was usually at midnight. When the bridegroom did come, he came with a shout (Matthew 25:6) and with the blowing of a *shofar* (trumpet) (1 Thessalonians 4:16-17; Revelation 4:1). The marriage between the bride and the groom will take place under the *chupah* or wedding canopy. Since Heaven is a type of *chupah*, we can see that when *Yeshua* gives a shout for His bride, accompanied by the blowing of a *shofar* (trumpet), the marriage between *Yeshua* and His bride will take place in Heaven.

The marriage ceremony will have a sacred procession. For this reason, the bridegroom (*Yeshua*) will be led to the *chupah* first. When the bridegroom approaches the *chupah*, the cantor chants, "Blessed is he who comes." "Blessed is he who comes" is an idiomatic expression meaning "welcome."

Yeshua said that He would not return for His bride until these words were said (Matthew 23:39). The groom is greeted like a king under the *chupah*. During this time *Yeshua*, the bridegroom, will be crowned King under the *chupah*, which is Heaven.

11. **He would abduct his bride, usually in the middle of the night, to go to the bridal chamber where the marriage would be consummated. This is the full marriage, known in Hebrew as *nesu'in*.**

The bride and groom will go to the wedding chamber, or *chadar* in Hebrew, where the marriage will be consummated. They will stay in that wedding chamber for seven days, or a week. At the end of the seven days, the bride and groom will come out from the wedding chamber. This can be seen in Joel 2:16.

The word *week* in Hebrew is *shavuah*. It means a "seven." It can mean seven days or seven years. An example of the Hebrew word for week (*shavuah*) meaning seven years can be found in Daniel 9:24, as it is written, "Seventy weeks [*shavuah*, 490 years] are determined upon thy people..." and in 9:27, "And he [the false Messiah known as the antichrist] shall confirm the covenant with many for one week [*shavuah*, seven years]...." The week referred to in Daniel 9:27 is known to Bible believers as the tribulation period. The Jewish people understand this time to be the birthpangs of the Messiah known in Hebrew eschatology as the *Chevlai shel Mashiach*. This is taken from Jeremiah 30:5-7.

12. **Finally, there would be a marriage supper for all the guests invited by the father of the bride.**

The bride and the groom would be in the wedding chamber for seven days. When the bride and the groom initially went into the wedding chamber, the friend of the bridegroom stood outside the door. All the assembled guests of the wedding gathered outside, waiting for the friend of the bridegroom to announce the consummation of the marriage, which was relayed to him by the groom. John (*Yochanan*) the Immerser (Baptist) referred to this in John 3:29. At this signal, great rejoicing broke forth (John 3:29). The marriage was consummated on the first night (Genesis [*Bereishit*] 29:23). The bloodstained linen from this night was preserved. It was proof of the bride's virginity (Deuteronomy [*Devarim*] 22:13-21).

On the wedding day, the bridegroom is seen as a king and the bride as a queen. During the consummation of the marriage, the bridegroom (*Yeshua*) will be crowned King over all the earth and the bride (the believers in *Yeshua*, the Messiah) will live with Him and rule with Him forever. The crowning of the King and the marriage can be seen in Isaiah 62:3-7. At the end of the week (seven-year tribulation, or birthpangs of the Messiah), the marriage supper will take place. The marriage supper will not take place in Heaven. After the marriage, the bride and Groom will return to earth. The marriage supper will be taking place on earth and only the invited guests of the Father of the Groom (G-d the Father) will be present at the banquet meal. This can be seen in Revelation 19:7-16 and 20:4. *Yeshua* spoke of the marriage supper and the banquet in Luke 12:35-38 and Matthew 8:11. The wedding supper is a theme of the festival of *Sukkot*, which will be discussed further in a later chapter. During *Sukkot*, the people were instructed by G-d to build a temporary shelter. One of the things G-d instructed the people to do is eat there. When they eat, they are to set a plate for seven different people. Among the seven whom a plate is set for are Abraham (*Avraham*), Isaac (*Yitzchak*), and Jacob (*Ya'akov*). This is what *Yeshua* was referring to in Matthew 8:11.

The unbelievers in the Messiah will attend a separate banquet where the fowls of the air will eat their flesh. This can be seen in Revelation 19:17-18.

The home of the bride was Jerusalem and it was the bridegroom who came to the bride to dwell with her. It is from Jerusalem that the believers in the Messiah during the Messianic age, or Millennium, will reign with the Messiah. This can be seen in Revelation 21:1-3; Ezekiel 43:1-2,7; Isaiah 2:2-4; Micah 4:1-5; and Zechariah 2:10-12.[30]

In concluding this section on the wedding, whenever anyone hears the message of the *basar* (gospel), it is a wedding proposal by G-d to accept Him and be a part of His bride. G-d desires that we accept His invitation and give Him our response of "I do." In fact, Revelation 22:20 is a proposal by *Yeshua* Himself to accept Him and be a part of His bride. His message in this verse is "Come." Will you say, "I do" to the Messiah's proposal to you?

The Resurrection of the Dead

One of the reasons for blowing the *shofar* is to proclaim the resurrection of the dead. In addition, the thirteenth principle of the Jewish faith is belief in the resurrection of the dead. The resurrection of the dead will take place on *Rosh HaShanah* (Talmud, Rosh HaShanah 16b). In First Corinthians 15:52, the apostle Paul (*Rav Sha'ul*) tells us that the resurrection of the dead will be "at the last trump." Earlier, in First Corinthians

15:14, he wrote that without the Messiah rising from the dead, our faith is in vain.

We cannot go to the Book of Revelation and say that the voice of the seventh angel (Revelation 11:15) is the last trump. In the first century, the last trump (*shofar*) meant a specific day in the year. In Judaism, there are three trumpets (*shofarim*) that have a name. They are the first trump, the last trump, and the great trump. Each one of these trumpets indicates a specific day in the Jewish year. The first trump is blown on the Feast of *Shavuot* (Pentecost) (Exodus [*Shemot*] 19:19). It proclaimed that G-d had betrothed Himself to Israel. The last trump is synonymous with *Rosh HaShanah*, according to Theodore Gaster in his book, *Festivals of the Jewish Year*, in his chapter on *Rosh HaShanah*. Herman Kieval also states the same thing in his book, *The High Holy Days* (Volume I, *Rosh HaShanah*, Chapter 5, Footnote 11), in the chapter on the *shofar*. The great trumpet is blown on *Yom Kippur*, which will herald the return of the Messiah *Yeshua* back to earth (Matthew [*Mattityahu*] 24:31).

The first and last trump relate to the two horns of the ram, which according to Jewish tradition, was caught in the thicket on Mount Moriah when Abraham (*Avraham*) was ready to slay Isaac (*Yitzchak*) and offer him up as a burnt offering (*olah*). This ram became the substitute for Isaac (*Yitzchak*) even as *Yeshua* became the substitute for us and provided life for us through His death.

In *Pirkei Avot* (the sayings of the fathers), Rabbi Eliezer tells us that the left horn (first trump) was blown on Mount Sinai, and its right horn (the last trump) will be blown to herald the coming of the Messiah. Isaiah (*Yeshayahu*) 18:3 and First Thessalonians 4:13-18 speak of the resurrection of the dead. First Thessalonians chapter 5 continues with the day of the L-rd and the birthpangs of the Messiah. First Thessalonians 4:16-17 says that the dead in Messiah will rise first, and that the catching away of the believers will immediately follow.

The term *rapture* comes from the Greek word *harpazo*, which means "to seize, catch away, catch up, pluck, pull, take by force" (1 Thessalonians 4:17). The Hebrew equivalent is the word *natzal*. Isaiah (*Yeshayahu*) 26:2-3, 19-20 and 57:1-2 all speak clearly of the resurrection of the dead. Daniel 12:1-2 also speaks of the resurrection of the dead, the tribulation, and the salvation of Israel through the tribulation. Zephaniah 1:14-18 and 2:2-3 tells about the terrible times during the day of the L-rd, the birthpangs of the Messiah, and issues a decree to repent and turn to G-d before that day to be hid from that time. Psalm (*Tehillim*) 27:5 says the righteous will be hid in the time of trouble. This psalm is read every day during the 40-day period of *Teshuvah*. Second Thessalonians 2:1 says, "Now we beseech you, brethren, by the coming of our Lord Jesus Christ, and by our gathering together unto Him." The phrase, "gathering together" comes from the Greek word *episunagoge*, which means "an assembly." In Numbers (*Bamidbar*) 10:2-3, the trumpet is blown to assemble the people. The blowing of the trumpet and the assembling of the people also appear together in First Thessalonians 4:16-17 and First Corinthians 15:51-53.[31]

Yom HaKeseh: The Hidden Day

In Psalm (*Tehillim*) 27:5 it is written, "For in the time of trouble He shall *hide* me in His pavilion; in the secret of His tabernacle shall He *hide* me; He shall set me up upon a rock."

Yet another name for *Rosh HaShanah* is *Yom HaKeseh*, "The Day of the Hiding" or "the Hidden Day." The term *ke-seh* or *keceh* is derived from the Hebrew root *kacah*, which means to "conceal, cover, or hide." Every day during the month of Elul, a trumpet is blown to warn the people to turn back to G-d, except for the thirtieth day of Elul, the day preceding *Rosh HaShanah*. On that day the trumpet is not blown, and is therefore silent. This is because much about *Rosh HaShanah* is concealed and shrouded in mystery. The mystical aspect of *Rosh HaShanah* is indicated in Scripture: "Sound the shofar on the New Moon, in concealment of the day of our festival" (Psalm [*Tehillim*] 81:3).[32] Satan, the accuser, is not to be given notice about the arrival of *Rosh HaShanah*, the Day of Judgment.[33]

Rosh HaShanah is called *Yom HaKeseh*, or the Day of the Hiding, because it was hidden from satan (*Ha satan*), the adversary. The Bible says that satan comes to rob and to steal (John [*Yochanan*] 10:10), and to confuse (1 Corinthians 14:33). Because it is the Day of Judgment, it is symbolically hidden from satan (satan did not know and understand the plan of the cross [tree], First Corinthians 2:7-8). This was hidden from him as well. Believers never said when the day of *Rosh HaShanah* was; they simply said, "Of that day and hour no one knows, only the Father."[34]

One of the reasons most often given to disclaim that the resurrection of the dead and the catching away of the believers is on *Rosh HaShanah* is the statement given by *Yeshua* in Matthew (*Mattityahu*) 24:36, as it is written, "But of that day and hour knoweth no man, no, not the angels of heaven, but My Father only." Because *Rosh HaShanah* was understood to be *the* hidden day, this statement by *Yeshua* is actually an idiom for *Rosh HaShanah*. Thus it should be given as proof that He was speaking of *Rosh HaShanah* because *Rosh Ha-Shanah* is the only day in the whole year that was referred to as *the* hidden day or the day that no man knew.

Spiritual Application (Halacha). *Rosh HaShanah* takes place on the new moon. Colossians 2:16-17 says that the new moon will teach about the Messiah. The Jewish (biblical) month is based upon a lunar cycle. The moon can barely be seen as the cycle begins. But then the moon turns toward the sun and begins to reflect the light of the sun. The sun in the sky is a picture of *Yeshua* (Malachi [*Malachie*] 4:2), and the moon is a picture of the believers in the Messiah. The sun has its own light, but the moon's light is a reflection of the sun. When we first become believers in *Yeshua*, we can hardly be seen spiritually, and we know very little about G-d. But then our lives begin to revolve around the Messiah as the moon revolves around the sun. As we begin to turn more and more toward the center of creation, we begin to reflect that light (*Yeshua*) more and more, just as the moon reflects the light from the center of the solar system.

Chapter 8

Yom Kippur:
The Day of Atonement

For it is on this day that atonement shall be made for you to cleanse you; and you shall be clean from all your sins before the Lord. It is to be a sabbath of solemn rest for you, that you may humble your souls; it is a permanent statute (Leviticus [*Vayikra*] 16:30-31 NAS).

On exactly the tenth day of this seventh month is the day of atonement...for it is a day of atonement, to make atonement on your behalf before the Lord your God. ... You shall do no work at all. It is to be a perpetual statute throughout your generations in all your dwelling places. It is to be a sabbath of complete rest to you, and you shall humble your souls; on the ninth of the month at evening, from evening until evening you shall keep your sabbath (Leviticus [*Vayikra*] 23:27-28,31-32 NAS).

Then on the tenth day of this seventh month you shall have a holy convocation, and you shall humble yourselves; you shall not do any work (Numbers [*Bamidbar*] 29:7 NAS).

Yom Kippur: **Names, Themes, and Idioms**

1. *Yom Kippur* (the Day of Atonement)
2. Face to Face
3. *The* Day (or the Great Day)
4. The Fast
5. The Great *Shofar* (*Shofar HaGadol*)
6. *Neilah* (the closing of the gates)

Understanding the Priestly Service for *Yom Kippur*

Leviticus (*Vayikra*) chapter 16, specifies the tenth of Tishrei as the date on which the high priest (*Cohen Ha-Gadol*) shall conduct a special ceremony to purge defilement from the shrine and from the people. The heart of the ritual is that the high priest (*Cohen HaGadol*) shall bring a bull and two goats as a special offering. First, the bull is sacrificed to purge the shrine from any defilements (what might now be called uncanny vibrations) caused by misdeeds of the priest himself and of his household (Leviticus [*Vayikra*] 16:6). Secondly, one of the goats is chosen by lot to be sacrificed to purge the shrine of any similar defilement stimulated by misdeeds of the whole Israelite people (Leviticus [*Vayikra*] 16:7-8). Finally, the second goat is sent away, not sacrificed, to cleanse the people themselves. The goat is marked for *Azazel* and is sent away to wander in the wilderness (Leviticus [*Vayikra*] 16:10). Before the goat is sent out, the high priest lays both his hands upon its head and confesses over it all the iniquities and transgressions of the Israelites, whatever their misdeeds, and so putting them on the head of the goat. Thus, the Torah adds, "The goat shall carry on it all their iniquities to an inaccessible region..." (Leviticus [*Vayikra*] 16:20-22).[1]

Azazel: The Scapegoat

The Hebrew word for scapegoat is *azazel*. *Azazel* was seen as a type of satan (*Ha satan*) in the intertestamental Book of Enoch (8:1).[2] The sins of the people and thus the punishment of the people were laid upon *azazel*, the scapegoat. He would bear the sins of the people and the punishment of the people would be upon him. *Azazel* being sent into the wilderness is understood to be a picture of satan (*Ha satan*) being cast into the lake of fire (Revelation 19:20).

Let's take a closer look at this ceremony found in Leviticus (*Vayikra*) 16:7-10. In Leviticus (*Vayikra*) 16:8, the first lot said, "*La Adonai*" (To the L-rd). The second lot said, "*La Azazel*" (To the scapegoat). The high priest (*Cohen Ha-Gadol*) took the two golden lots, one marked *La Adonai* and the other marked *La Azazel,* and placed one upon the head of each animal, sealing their fate. It was considered a good omen if the lot marked *La Adonai* was drawn by the priest in the right hand, but for 40 years prior to the destruction of the temple (*Beit HaMikdash*) in 70 C.E. (Common Era, which is the same as A.D., the Latin for "in the year of our L-rd"), the lot *La Adonai* was drawn by the priest on the left hand (Talmud, Yoma 39a). In any event, the sins of the people were laid upon the scapegoat (Leviticus [*Vayikra*] 16:21-22). Except for the 40 years prior to the destruction of the second temple (*Beit HaMikdash*), the lot *La Adonai* came out on the right hand of the priest and the lot *La Azazel* came out on the left hand of the priest.

Messianic Understanding

G-d gave this ceremony of the casting of lots during *Yom Kippur* to teach us how He will judge the nations of the world prior to the Messianic age known as the Millennium. The nations of the world will be judged according to how they treated the Jewish people. Those nations who mistreated the Jews will be goat nations and they will go into the left hand. Those nations that stood beside the Jewish people will be sheep nations and will enter into the Messianic kingdom or the Millennium. *Yeshua* taught us about this in Matthew 25:31-46.

Yeshua during His first coming was a type of the goat marked *La Adonai*. *Yeshua* was a sin offering to us as G-d laid upon Him the sins of the whole world (Isaiah [*Yeshayahu*] 53:1-6; 1 Corinthians 15:3; Galatians 1:3-4; Hebrews 2:17; 1 John [*Yochanan*] 2:2; 4:10).

In the ceremony of the two goats, the two goats were considered as one offering. A crimson sash was tied around the horns of the goat marked *azazel*. At the appropriate time, the goat was led to a steep cliff in the wilderness and shoved off the cliff. In connection with this ceremony, an interesting tradition arose that is mentioned in the Mishnah. A portion of the crimson sash was attached to the door of the temple (*Beit HaMikdash*) before the goat was sent into the wilderness. The sash would turn from red to white as the goat met its end, signaling to the people that G-d had accepted their sacrifices and their sins were forgiven. This was based upon Isaiah (*Yeshayahu*) 1:18. As stated earlier, the Mishnah tells us that 40 years before the destruction of the temple (*Beit*

HaMikdash), the sash stopped turning white. This, of course, was when *Yeshua* was slain on the tree.[3]

Additional Aspects to the High Priest Ceremony

In order to enter the Holy of Holies, the high priest (*Cohen HaGadol*) was first to bathe his entire body, going beyond the mere washing of hands and feet as required by other occasions. The washing symbolized his desire for purification (Numbers [*Bamidbar*] 19).[4] The washing was of his clothes and his flesh (Numbers [*Bamidbar*] 8:5-7; 19:7-9). This was done in conjunction with taking the blood of an animal with the finger and sprinkling the blood upon the altar (Numbers [*Bamidbar*] 19:1-4; Leviticus [*Vayikra*] 8:13-15). This ritual is once again seen in Numbers (*Bamidbar*) 31:21-24. The spiritual understanding of this is given in Hebrews 9; and 10:19-22. The sprinkling of blood upon the altar is also mentioned in Exodus (*Shemot*) 29:1-4,10-12, 16,20-21; and Leviticus (*Vayikra*) 1:3-5,11; 3:1-2,8; 4:1-6; 5:4-6,9. Once again, the spiritual understanding is found in Hebrews 9:11-14,23-25, and First Peter (*Kefa*) 1:2.

Messianic Understanding

Yeshua is the High Priest (*Cohen HaGadol*) of G-d (Hebrews 3:1). In John (*Yochanan*) 20:17, *Yeshua* said, "Touch Me not; for I am not yet ascended to My Father...." These were the same words that the priest spoke before he ascended the altar. *Yeshua* can be seen as Priest by looking at some other Scriptures. In Numbers (*Bamidbar*) 19:11, if you touched a dead body, you were unclean for seven days. After being unclean, purification took place on the eighth day. This is the meaning behind what happened in John (*Yochanan*) 20:24-27.

Rather than wearing his usual robe and colorful garments (described in Exodus [*Shemot*] 28 and Leviticus [*Vayikra*] 8:1-8), Aaron was commanded to wear special garments of linen (Leviticus [*Vayikra*] 16:4). *Yeshua* was seen wearing the same thing in Revelation 1:13-15. Daniel also saw this and described it in Daniel 10:5-6.

By slaying the animals at the altar and applying their blood to the altar, the garments of the high priest became very bloody and G-d instructed them to be washed (Leviticus [*Vayikra*] 6:27). However, on *Yom Kippur* G-d declared in Isaiah (*Yeshayahu*) 1:18, as it is written, "...though your sins be as scarlet, they shall be as white as snow...." Spiritually speaking, a white garment represents purity and the absence of sin (Revelation 7:9,13-14; 19:8).

In Numbers (*Bamidbar*) 15:37-41, fringes (*tzit-tzit*) were put on the hem of the garments to remind the people of the Torah or G-d's Word. Consider the woman with the issue of blood (she was unclean) coming to *Yeshua* (the High Priest of G-d) to touch the hem of His garment and be healed (Matthew [*Mattityahu*] 9:20-22). The children of Israel were instructed by G-d to wear the garments *Yeshua* had on in Matthew 9:20-22. These garments were instructed by G-d in the Torah to be worn as just stated in Numbers (*Bamidbar*) 15:37-41. When the woman with the issue of blood touched the hem (*tzit-tzit*) of *Yeshua's* garment in Matthew 9:20-22, it was a picture given to us by G-d to communicate to us that she believed *Yeshua's* word by faith (*emunah*) and was made well because of her faith.

Face to Face

The high priest (*Cohen HaGadol*) could only go into the Holy of Holies once a year (Leviticus [*Vayikra*] 16:2; Hebrews 9:6-7). G-d issued a warning that no man could see His face and live (Exodus [*Shemot*] 33:20). But because on the Day of Atonement the priest could be in G-d's presence (Leviticus [*Vayikra*] 16:2), another term for the Day of Atonement is "face to face."

By the time of the second temple, this ritual (the high priest's [*Cohen HaGadol*] ceremony) had been somewhat elaborated, and one crucial element had been added to it. That element was that on three separate occasions, in a grand crescendo, the high priest appeared before the people, and three times he recited a formula of confession in their hearing. The first confession was on the account of his own sins and those of his household; the second, on the account of the priestly tribe of Levi; the third, on the account of the whole people.

On this occasion only, in the entire year, the confession included the priest's saying aloud the name of G-d embodied in the Hebrew letters YHVH (called the Tetragrammaton). This was the name that G-d gave and explained to Moses (*Moshe*) at the burning bush, the name that was a kind of distillation of "I am Becoming Who I am Becoming," the name that was not a name in the sense of a label by which G-d could be called and controlled, and therefore the name that could not be said aloud. It was, therefore, all year long euphemized by saying, whenever YHVH appeared in the text, or invocation, *Adonai*, The L-rd. Only on *Yom Kippur* was the name said, aloud, in all its original awesomeness.

(How the name was pronounced on this occasion was so thoroughly protected from record-keeping, that might profane it, that we no longer know how it was done.)

In each confession, when the high priest reached the recitation of the name, the whole people would prostrate themselves and say aloud, "*Baruch shem K'vod malchuto l'olam va'ed*," which means, "Blessed be the Name of the radiance of the Kingship, forever and beyond." On the third recitation, the one for their own sins, they knew that the high priest (*Cohen HaGadol*) had just before—on this one occasion in all the year—entered the Holy of Holies, the inmost room of the temple (*Beit HaMikdash*) where G-d's Presence was most fully felt. He entered it three times, and only then came out to confess on behalf of all the people and put their sins upon the head of the goat for *azazel*.

The result of this triple entry into the Holy of Holies, this triple recitation of G-d's most holy name, and this triple prostration by the entire people, was an utterly awesome sense of G-d's Presence making atonement for the people, cleansing them of all their sins, permitting them to begin the year afresh, renewing their lives. So total was this sense of transformation that, after it, the mood of the people shifted from solemn awe to joyful celebration. The young, unmarried men and women went to dance in the fields and to choose spouses for themselves. *Yom Kippur* and the fifteenth of Av were the only days in the year when this kind of mass public espousal would take place.[5]

Therefore, when the high priest stood before G-d on this day, he was said to be "face to face" with G-d. Because of this, *Yom Kippur* became known by the phrase "face to face."

"Face to face" terminology was used in First Corinthians 13:9-12, as it is written:

For we know in part, and we prophesy in part. But when that which is perfect is come, then that which is in part shall be done away. When I was a child, I spake as a child, I understood as a child, I thought as a child: but when I became a man, I put away child-ish things. For now we see through a glass, darkly; but then face to face: now I know in part; but then shall I know even as also I am known (1 Corinthians 13:9-12).

Both verse 11 and the phrase in verse 12, "For now we see through a glass, darkly" come from the Jewish Midrash.

"Face to Face" is the title of a chapter in Arthur Waskow's book, *Seasons of Our Joy*, on the topic of *Yom Kippur*. "Face to face" is an idiom for *Yom Kippur*. Why? It was on *Yom Kippur* that the high priest had to go behind the veil of the temple. At that moment, the nation had to hold its breath be-cause the nation's fate depended upon G-d's accepting the sacrifice. At that point, the high priest was "face to face with the mercy seat of G-d."[6]

When the high priest (*Cohen HaGadol*) entered the Holy of Holies, he saw the L-rd's presence as a brilliant cloud hov-ering above the mercy seat (Leviticus [*Vayikra*] 16:2). The word for mercy seat in Hebrew is *kapporet*. It comes from the root word *kaphar*, which is the same word used for "atonement." The mercy seat can also be translated as the seat of atonement. The mercy seat is described in detail in Exodus (*Shemot*) 25:17-22 and 37:6-9. This is the place where Moses (*Moshe*) met and spoke with G-d face to face (Exodus [*Shemot*] 25:22; 30:6; Numbers [*Bamidbar*] 7:89).

The Day

Yom Kippur, the Day of Atonement, comes on the tenth day of the Jewish month of Tishrei (September/October). It is the last day of the Ten Days of Repentance, and it is the most solemn day of the Jewish calendar. It is believed that those who have not been good enough to be written in the Book of Life immediately on *Rosh HaShanah* are given ten days to repent, pray for forgiveness, and do good deeds until *Yom Kippur*, when their fate will be decided. The entire Day of Forgiveness (*Yom Kippur*) is spent fasting and praying.[7] Because this day is the most solemn day in the year, it is known as "The Day."

The Fast

Fasting is one of the most important of the *mitzvot* (commandments) leading to atonement. The Torah says three times, "And this shall be to you a law for all times: In the seventh month, on the tenth day of the month you shall practice self-denial" (Leviticus [*Vayikra*] 16:29; 23:27; Numbers [*Bamidbar*] 29:7); tradition (the Jewish understanding) interprets self-denial as fasting.[8] For this reason, *Yom Kippur* is known as "The Fast Day."

The Great *Shofar*

As mentioned earlier in this book in Chapter 7, when the *shofar* (trumpet) was discussed, there are three primary *shofarim* (trumpets) to the Jewish people and these three trumpets are associated with specific days in the year. These three trumpets are: (a) "The First Trump," blown and associated with *Shavuot* (Pentecost); (b) "The Last Trump," blown and associated with *Rosh HaShanah*; (c) "The Great Trump," blown and associated with *Yom Kippur*. It is on *Yom Kippur* when the Great Trumpet, known in Hebrew as the *Shofar HaGadol* is blown. This is referred to in Isaiah (*Yeshayahu*) 27:13 and Matthew 24:31.

Neilah: The Closing of the Gates of Heaven

Neilah is the closing or final service of *Yom Kippur*. It is the Jewish belief that the gates of Heaven are open during the days of repentance to receive our prayers for forgiveness and that they close after the *neilah* service.[9] (Specifically, they are open on *Rosh HaShanah* to let the righteous into Heaven and remain open until the *neilah* service of *Yom Kippur*.) When the final blast of the *shofar* (the *Shofar HaGadol*, the Great Trumpet) is heard at the end of the *neilah* service, those who have observed the day with sincerity should feel that they have been inscribed and sealed in the Book of Life.[10]

Spiritual Understanding of the Day of Atonement

The Day of Atonement was the most solemn of all the feast days. It was the day of cleansing for the nation and for the sanctuary. On this day alone, once a year, the high priest entered into the holiest of all, the Holy of Holies in the temple, within the veil of the temple, with the blood of the L-rd's goat, the sin offering. Here he sprinkled the blood on the mercy seat. The blood of the sin offering on the great Day of Atonement brought about the cleansing of all sin for the priesthood, the sanctuary, and Israel as a nation (Leviticus [*Vayikra*] 16:29-34).

The Day of Atonement

1. ***Yom Kippur* is a day of fasting and affliction of the soul** (Leviticus [*Vayikra*] 23:27,29; Numbers [*Bamidbar*] 29:7). This day was set aside as a day of national fasting. Fasting is mentioned in Joel (*Yoel*) 1:14-15; 2:12-18; and Ezra 8:21. The spiritual understanding for us is given in Isaiah 58:1-12.

2. **It is the tenth day of the seventh month** (Leviticus [*Vayikra*] 23:27; Numbers [*Bamidbar*] 29:7). The number ten is used to represent the government or a nation (Daniel 7:24; Revelation 17:12). To the Jewish people, the number ten represents a legal congregation known as a *minyan*. The congregation is one body that can represent a group. So, the number ten represented the nation or the congregation of Israel (Leviticus [*Vayikra*] 16:2-3,17,19). Notice also that the blood is sprinkled for the nation (Leviticus [*Vayikra*] 16:19). Look at Isaiah (*Yeshayahu*) 52:13-15 and Ezekiel (*Yechezekel*) 36:24-26.

In Isaiah (*Yeshayahu*) 52:13-15, the suffering servant, *Yeshua*, Messiah ben Joseph (*Yosef*) is seen sprinkling many nations. In Ezekiel 36:24-26, it is the Jews returning to Israel from the Diaspora whom G-d will sprinkle clean water upon when they return back to the land of Israel.

The Day of Atonement Ceremonies

As we look at the ceremony itself, we will be able to see how it points to the Messiah *Yeshua* Himself. In addition, we will be able to see how it relates to the believers in the Messiah.

1. **The priest used a golden censer** (Leviticus 16:1-2,12-14; Hebrews 9:4). The censer is mentioned in Leviticus 16:12; Numbers 16:18,46; First Kings 7:50-51; Second Chronicles 4:19,22; and Hebrews 9:1,4.

    Spiritual Application (Halacha). The incense of the golden censer represents the prayers of Bible believers (Psalm 141:2; Luke 1:5-11; Revelation 5:8; 8:3-4).

    Messianic Fulfillment. Aaron the high priest typifies the ministry of mediator and intercessor. *Yeshua* is our High Priest (Hebrews 3:1) and Mediator (1 Timothy 2:5; Hebrews 12:24). He lives to make intercession for us (Romans 8:34; Hebrews 7:22-27).

2. **He went within the veil once a year** (Leviticus 16:2; Hebrews 9:3,7).

    Spiritual Application (Halacha). By the death of *Yeshua*, we are free to enter into the veil every day (Matthew 27:50-51; 2 Corinthians 3:14; Hebrews 4:16; 6:13-19; 10:19-22).

3. **He washed himself in water** (Leviticus [*Vayikra*] 16:4,24).

    Spiritual Application (Halacha). For Aaron, this meant he must be absolutely clean in order to make atonement in behalf of the people of Israel. For the believer in *Yeshua*, it means we are to be washed by the water of the Word of G-d as we approach G-d as well for the removal of sin from our lives (John 3:1-5,15; 1 Corinthians 6:11; Ephesians 5:26-27; Titus 3:5; Hebrews 10:22). For *Yeshua,* it meant that He was absolutely clean and without sin when He made the atonement of sacrificing His body on the tree.

4. **He put on holy linen garments** (Leviticus [*Vayikra*] 16:4,23).

    Spiritual Application (Halacha). The priestly clothing is also mentioned in Exodus (*Shemot*) 28:1-4. In verse 2 they are for glory and beauty. The linen garments speak of the sinless humanity of Messiah and His righteousness. These linen garments were stained with blood while the priest offered the sacrifices. After the sacrifices were complete, the garments were taken off and new garments were put on again (Leviticus [*Vayikra*] 16:23-24). Isaiah (*Yeshayahu*) 1:18 speaks of the blood-stained garments and the new garments that were put on afterwards. The white linen garments are clothes of righteousness (Job [*Iyov*] 29:14; Psalm [*Tehillim*] 132:9; Isaiah [*Yeshayahu*] 61:10; Revelation 3:5; 15:6; 19:7-8, 11,13-15).

5. **At the moment the atonement was made on the Day of Atonement, those being atoned for were sinless and blameless before G-d.** The congregation of believers (*kehilat*) in the Messiah is being presented before G-d without spot or blemish (Ephesians 5:27) because of the blood of *Yeshua* (1 Peter [*Kefa*] 1:19).

6. **The bodies of the animals were outside the camp** (Leviticus 16:27).

    Messianic Fulfillment. The bodies of the sin offering, both the bullock and the goat, were taken outside the camp where they were burned. *Yeshua* was crucified outside the camp or gates of Jerusalem (John 19:17-20; Hebrews 13:10-13).

7. **Many sacrifices were offered** (Leviticus 16:1-6,25-27).

   Spiritual Application (Halacha). Our bodies are to be a living sacrifice to G-d (Romans 12:1; 1 Peter [*Kefa*] 2:5). We are to offer up a sacrifice of praise to G-d (Leviticus [*Vayikra*] 7:12; Psalm [*Tehillim*] 34:1; 50:14,23; 69:30-31; 107:22; 116:17; Hebrews 13:15-16).

   Messianic Fulfillment. *Yeshua* is the sacrifice of G-d for us who believe on Him (Hebrews 9:26-28; 10:1-10).

8. **The year of Jubilee was the Day of Atonement** (Leviticus 25:9-11).

   Spiritual Application (Halacha). This was a year and day of liberty. *Yeshua* came to preach this liberty at His first coming (Isaiah [*Yeshayahu*] 61:1-3; Luke 4:17-21). From Adam, it has been almost 6,000 years and 120 Jubilees. The number 120 points to the end of the age of the flesh and the reign of the life of the spirit (Genesis [*Bereishit*] 6:3). The ultimate fulfillment of the year of Jubilee will take place at the second coming of Messiah. The earth will be redeemed and come into full and complete rest from the curse brought upon it by Adam's sin. Complete restoration of man's lost inheritance will take place. G-d's people will be totally set free—set at liberty, from all sin, sickness and disease, death, and the curse. Satan (*Ha satan*), the source of all these things, will be bound and true rest will be realized. The tabernacle of G-d will be with men and He will dwell with them

(Revelation 21:1-4). So, the year of Jubilee and the day of Atonement speak of the fullness of the redemptive plan of G-d for man.[11]

Life for a Life

The biblical name for the Day of Atonement is *Yom HaKippurim*, meaning "the day of covering, canceling, pardon, reconciling." Occasionally, it was called "the Day of the Fast" or "the Great Fast" (Leviticus [*Vayikra*] 23:27-31; 16:29-34).

G-d told the Israelites to sacrifice an animal as a substitute for their own sentence to die. This life for a life principle is the foundation of the sacrificial system. The Torah allows a monetary ransom be paid for an individual deserving death (Exodus [*Shemot*] 21:28-32). The guilty person here was the owner of an ox that had killed a person, and the owner of the ox was responsible for the death caused by his ox (Exodus 21:30 says that money paid in place of the death of the owner was a ransom price).[12]

Messianic Fulfillment. *Yeshua* died on the tree as a substitute for us, who deserved death because we sinned against G-d. *Yeshua* paid the ransom price for us to G-d (Mark 10:45; 1 Timothy 2:5-6; 1 Corinthians 6:20; 7:23). The ransom price was 30 pieces of silver (Exodus [*Shemot*] 21:32; Matthew [*Mattityahu*] 26:14-16; 27:3-6).

Thirty pieces of silver was the ransom price of blood in dying in the place of the truly guilty and making atonement for the guilty. In the case of a thief or murderer, there is no atonement for them (Exodus 22:1-2; Numbers 35:31). This is why there is no atonement for satan (*Ha satan*) (John 8:44). Thirty pieces of silver was the ransom price of blood and the shedding of blood made an atonement for sin (Leviticus 17:11; Romans 5:8-11). The Greek word *hilasmos*, translated as "propitiation," has the same meaning as the Hebrew word *kaphar*, which is translated as "atonement" (Romans 3:23-25; 1 John 2:2; 4:9-10). The purpose of the Day of Atonement was to teach us about *Yeshua*, who is our atonement (Hebrews 10:1-10).

The Significance of Blood in the Bible

1. **It is a token of the New Covenant** (*Brit Hadashah*) (Matthew [*Mattityahu*] 26:27-28; 1 Corinthians 11:25).
2. **It gives eternal life** (John [*Yochanan*] 6:53-54).
3. **It brings redemption** (Ephesians 1:7).
4. **It makes atonement** (Romans 3:25; 1 John 2:2; 4:9-10).
5. **It justifies before G-d** (Romans 5:9).
6. **It gives us forgiveness** (Ephesians 1:7; 2:13; Colossians 1:14; 1 John 1:9).
7. **It provides reconciliation** (Colossians 1:19-20).
8. **It provides cleansing** (1 John 1:7).
9. **It makes us overcomers** (Revelation 12:11).

The Day of Atonement is the tenth day of Tishrei (Leviticus [*Vayikra*] 23:27). It is significant that repentance (the season of *Teshuvah*) must precede redemption (*Yom Kippur*). G-d purposed that animal sacrifices were only appropriate when presented with a contrite and repentant heart (Psalm [*Tehillim*] 51:16-19). With this in mind, the Day of Atonement was to be kept as a perpetual statute through-out all generations (Leviticus [*Vayikra*] 23:31).

G-d divinely placed *Yom Kippur* before the Feast of Tab-ernacles (*Sukkot*), which is called "The Season of Our Joy." The children of Israel (and all believers in the Messiah *Yeshua*) could only rejoice once they were redeemed and their sins forgiven.[13]

Yeshua's Second Coming and *Yom Kippur*

If you examine the Scriptures concerning the second coming of *Yeshua* back to earth, when He will set His foot upon the Mount of Olives (Zechariah 14:4), you will find that it uses *Yom Kippur* terminology. Here are a few examples.

The first example is in Isaiah (*Yeshayahu*) 52:13-15. First, let us examine Isaiah 52:13-14 so we can identify that this is referring to *Yeshua* the Messiah. Then, we will look at Isaiah 52:15.

In Isaiah (*Yeshayahu*) 52:13-14 it is written:

Behold, My servant shall deal prudently [the servant refers to the Messiah], *He shall be exalted and ex-tolled, and be very high.* [The New Covenant (*Brit Hadashah*) references to this include Acts 2:32-35; 5:30-31; and Philippians 2:9-11.] *As many were aston-ied at thee; His visage was so marred more than any man, and His form more than the sons of men* (Isaiah [*Yeshayahu*] 52:13-14).

This description of *Yeshua*, the suffering Messiah, is dras-tically different from how *Yeshua* is portrayed in Hollywood.

This description depicts a lamb going to the slaughter (Isaiah 53:7). Isaiah (*Yeshayahu*) 52:14 depicts a man so marred that He did not resemble a man. Furthermore, Isaiah (*Yeshayahu*) 50:6 says that His beard was ripped out. Psalm (*Tehillim*) 22:14,17 says His bones were out of joint and that He was naked before the peering eyes of men. They even bit him (Psalm 22:13).

The Romans used a whip with nine strands, and each strand had bone, glass, and sharp metal in it. The purpose of the whip was to strip away the flesh so the organs would hang out of the body. Psalm 22:16 says they also pierced His hands and feet. Psalm 22:18 says they gambled for His garments. Recognizing that Isaiah 52:13-14 is speaking about *Yeshua* during His first coming to earth, Isaiah 52:15 will speak about His second coming.

In Isaiah (*Yeshayahu*) 52:15 it is written, "So shall He sprinkle many nations; the kings shall shut their mouths at Him: for that which had not been told them shall they see; and that which they had not heard shall they consider." The phrase, "So shall He sprinkle many nations" is a reference to the sprinkling of the blood on the mercy seat of G-d by the high priest during *Yom Kippur* (Leviticus 16:14). This is also referred to in Leviticus 1:5,11; 3:2,8,13; 4:6,17; 7:2.

The garments of the high priest were covered with blood after he had performed this task (Leviticus 6:27). After this, G-d accepted the sacrifice, and as the high priest hung out his garments, a miracle took place. His garments turned from bloodstained red to white.

G-d was saying in this that He had forgiven their sins and this forgiveness was shown by the garment (symbolic of man's life), being sprinkled upon by blood (the blood of *Yeshua*), *Yeshua* forgiving man's sins, and thus his garment turning white. Isaiah the prophet wrote, "Come now, and let us reason together, saith the Lord: though your sins be as scarlet, they shall be as white as snow; though they be red like crimson, they shall be as wool" (Isaiah 1:18).

Yeshua's garment went from being stained from His blood when He died upon the tree to being pure white today. White garments represent righteousness before G-d (Revelation 3:4-5; 7:9,13-14). *Yeshua* is described this way in Revelation 1:13-14. *Yeshua* is our High Priest (Hebrews 2:17; 3:1; 4:14; 9:11). *Yeshua* sprinkled His blood for us (1 Peter [*Kefa*] 1:2).

Moses (*Moshe*) led the children of Israel out of Egypt by keeping the Passover and sprinkling the blood as found in the Torah and referenced in Hebrews 11:24-28. In fact, G-d promised to sprinkle Israel when they returned to the land of Israel from the Diaspora. This can be seen in Ezekiel 36:24-27.

In Isaiah 52:15, when it says that *Yeshua* would sprinkle the nations, it refers to what the high priest did on *Yom Kippur* on the mercy seat of G-d so G-d would forgive the sins of the people. *Yeshua* came as a prophet in His first coming; now He is the High Priest and is coming back as a King. Isaiah 63:1-3 describes the second coming of *Yeshua*, and verse 3 talks about His garments being sprinkled with blood. Once again this describes *Yeshua*, the High Priest coming back to earth on *Yom Kippur*.[14]

In Joel (*Yoel*) 2:15-16 it is written:

Blow the trumpet in Zion [the trumpet (*shofar*) spoken of here refers to the trumpet ushering in the Messianic

Kingdom, the last trump that is blown on *Rosh Ha-Shanah*] *sanctify a fast, call a solemn assembly* [this speaks of the fast associated with *Yom Kippur*]: *gather the people, sanctify the congregation, assemble the elders, gather the children, and those that suck the breasts: let the bridegroom go forth of his chamber, and the bride out of her closet* (Joel [*Yoel*] 2:15-16).

Please refer back to the previous chapter on the wedding that takes place on *Rosh HaShanah* and the honeymoon. In this passage in Joel, we can see that the seven years of the tribulation, known as the birthpangs of the Messiah or *Chevlai shel Mashiach*, are over and the Messiah is coming back with His followers to go to the marriage supper of the Lamb.

In Joel 2:17 it is written:

Let the priests, the ministers of the Lord, weep between the porch and the altar [once again, this speaks of an event that took place annually, the priest ministering in the Holy of Holies], *and let them say, Spare Thy people, O Lord, and give not Thine heritage to reproach, that the heathen should rule over them: wherefore should they say among the people, Where is their God?* (Joel [*Yoel*] 2:17)

What is being communicated here by the phrase "spare Thy people"? For the answer we must turn to Zechariah 12 and 14:1-9. In these passages, we can see *Yeshua* coming back after the birthpangs of the Messiah (tribulation), and Jerusalem (*Yerushalayim*) about to be under siege. *Yeshua* saves Jerusalem (*Yerushalayim*). His feet are placed on the

Mount of Olives. There is a great earthquake, and the Messianic Kingdom comes in full power. There is no nighttime anymore, and the L-rd will rule the whole earth. At this time, the gates of Heaven are closed. The last *Yom Kippur* ceremony is called *neilah*, the closing of the gates, and is the concluding ceremony to *Yom Kippur*. However, this is not the rehearsal (*miqra*), but the real thing. At this point, it is too late to make a decision to accept *Yeshua* the Messiah into your life.

Yeshua spoke of this same event in Matthew (*Mattityahu*) 24:27-31. In Matthew 24:31, the trumpet that is being blown is called by *Yeshua* the great trumpet. This is the trumpet that is blown on *Yom Kippur* known as the *Shofar HaGadol*. This trumpet will usher the return of *Yeshua* to rule as Messiah ben David during the Messianic age.[15]

The themes of the fall feasts are numerous and are especially meaningful to the believer in *Yeshua*. The festivals and the entire Tanach (Old Testament) are fulfilled and speak about the Messiah (Psalm [*Tehillim*] 40:7; Luke 24:44-47). Understanding the fall festivals will enrich our lives and walk (*halacha*) as believers in the Messiah. The final fall festival, *Sukkot*, is no different. The festivals of the L-rd are fulfilled in *Yeshua* the Messiah while at the same time revealing tremendous insight on how to live for *Yeshua* on a daily basis. *Baruch Ha Shem!* Blessed be His Name!

Chapter 9

Sukkot:
The Feast of Tabernacles

*…On the fifteenth of this seventh month is the Feast of
Booths for seven days to the Lord* (Leviticus [*Vayikra*]
23:34 NAS).

*You shall celebrate the Feast of Booths seven days af-
ter you have gathered in* [the ingathering, KJV] *from
your threshing floor and your wine vat* (Deuteronomy
[*Devarim*] 16:13 NAS).

Sukkot, usually translated as "Tabernacles," or the festival of "Booths," occurs for seven days, from Tishrei 15 to
21. There is therefore a quick transition from the high holidays, with their somber mood of repentance and judgment, to a holiday of rejoicing and celebration, for which
the people are commanded to build a hut (*sukkah;* plural,
sukkot) and make it their home.[1] The Torah identifies
the *sukkah* (booth) with the temporary dwellings in
which the Israelites lived in the wilderness after they left
Egypt on their way to the Promised Land (Leviticus [*Vayikra*] 23:42).[2]

From *Yom Kippur* to *Sukkot*

Not coincidentally, the same time period marks the beginning of the construction of G-d's *sukkah*, the *mishkan*, the sanctuary in the desert (Exodus [*Shemot*] 25:8-9). In Exodus 25:9, the word *tabernacle* is the word *mishkan* in Hebrew. According to tradition, Moses (*Moshe*) again ascended Mount Sinai for 40 days and nights to receive the second set of tablets and descended on *Yom Kippur*, carrying them as a sign of G-d's forgiveness of Israel for the sin of the golden calf, and as a symbol of the lasting covenant between G-d and Israel (Exodus [*Shemot*] 24:12-18; 34:1-2; 27-28). The following day Moses (*Moshe*) relayed G-d's instructions for building the *mishkan*—a dwelling place. Material for this portable structure was collected during the days before *Sukkot*, and work was begun on it (the *mishkan* or tabernacle) (Exodus [*Shemot*] 35; 36:1-7).

Why was the *mishkan* built? The Torah says, "Let them make Me a sanctuary, that I may dwell among them" (Exodus [*Shemot*] 25:8); to establish the relationship between G-d and Israel, G-d would dwell amidst the people.[3] Therefore the *mishkan*, the tabernacle in the wilderness, was instructed to be built by G-d for Him so He could dwell with His people.

The *Sukkah* and the Clouds of Glory

The *Sukkah* reminds us of the clouds of glory that surrounded Israel during their wandering through the desert on the way to the Promised Land. Everybody then saw the special divine protection that G-d bestowed upon Israel during those difficult years.[4] As it is written in Exodus (*Shemot*) 13:21, "And the Lord was going before them in a pillar of cloud by day to lead them on the way, and in a pillar of fire by night to give them light, that they might travel by day and by night" (NAS).

Spiritual Application (Halacha). G-d desired that the tabernacle in the wilderness be built because He wanted to dwell with His people (Exodus [*Shemot*] 29:44-45). Spiritually speaking, this physical tabernacle was given by G-d to teach and instruct us that He desires to live and dwell with His people by means of the Holy Spirit (*Ruach HaKodesh*) (1 Corinthians 6:19; 2 Corinthians 6:1). The clouds represent the believers in *Yeshua* (Hebrews 12:1; Revelation 1:7).

Sukkot: Names, Themes, and Idioms

1. The Season of Our Joy
2. The Festival of Ingathering
3. The Feast of the Nations
4. The Festival of Dedication
5. The Festival of Lights

Understanding *Sukkot*: The Feast of Tabernacles

The Feast of Tabernacles (*Sukkot*) completes the sacred festivals of the seventh month. In contrast to the somber tone of *Rosh HaShanah* and the Day of Atonement, the third feast of Tishrei was a time of joy. Israel had passed through the season of repentance and redemption.[5]

Sukkot is called the "Season of Our Joy." One reason *Sukkot* was a time of joy was that after the season of repentance (*Teshuvah*) and the redemption of *Yom Kippur* came the joy of knowing your sins were forgiven and the joy of walking with G-d, knowing G-d, and being obedient to G-d. Historically, *Sukkot* commemorates the days in the wilderness of Sinai after coming out of Egypt (*Mitzrayim*). According to all natural laws, they (the Israelites) should have perished, but were instead divinely protected by G-d. Prophetically, *Sukkot* is the festival that teaches on the Messianic Kingdom and the joy of that Kingdom.

As mentioned earlier in this book, the Hebrew word *chag* comes from the Hebrew root word *chagag*, which means "to move in a circle, to march in a sacred procession, to celebrate or dance." The joy of *Sukkot* was so great that it became known as "The Feast." In non-Jewish circles, *Sukkot* is known as the Feast of Tabernacles. The word *tabernacle* refers to a temporary dwelling place, which is the purpose of the *sukkah*.

***Spiritual Application* (*Halacha*).** The *sukkah*, or booth, symbolizes man's need to depend upon G-d for his provision of food, water, and shelter. This is true in the spiritual realm as well. The booth is the physical body, which is a temporary dwelling place for our souls and spirits (1 Corinthians 6:19-20). We need the food that the Word of G-d provides (Matthew 4:4; 6:11; John 6:33-35); the cleansing, rinsing, and washing that the Word of G-d brings to our lives (Ephesians 5:26); and the shelter of G-d's protection over our lives from the evil one (Matthew 6:13; Psalm [*Tehillim*] 91). Our physical needs will be provided for by G-d if we seek Him spiritually (Matthew [*Mattityahu*] 6:31-33).

The observance of *Sukkot* described in Leviticus (*Vayikra*) 23:40-41 can be seen in Nehemiah (*Nechemiah*) chapter 8. The temporary dwellings or booths are described as a part of the festival. This is in remembrance of when the children of Israel dwelled in booths during their time in the wilderness (Leviticus [*Vayikra*] 23:43).

Isaiah talked about the *sukkah* in Isaiah (*Yeshayahu*) 4:4-6. The divine order declares that after judgment, *Yom Kippur* (Isaiah 4:4) comes *Sukkot* (Isaiah [*Yeshayahu*] 4:5-6). The command to rejoice at this time is given in Deuteronomy (*Devarim*) 16:13-15.

A *sukkah* is a temporary dwelling place. In First Kings (*Melachim*) 8:27 (NAS), at the dedication of Solomon's temple during the festival of *Sukkot*, Solomon asks, "Will God indeed dwell on the earth?"

The Scriptures say that *Yeshua* became flesh and dwelt (tabernacled) among us (John [*Yochanan*] 1:14). He came to earth at His first coming and temporarily dwelt among men.

The Covering of the *Sukkah*

Sukkot is a remembrance of the time in the wilderness when G-d protected, led, and sustained the children of Israel in the wilderness. The wilderness experience was a picture of the Millennium because there was a supernatural environment for the people in the wilderness. The covering was the cloud (Exodus [*Shemot*] 13:17-22; 14:16-20; 16:10; 19:1,9,16; 24:12-16; 40:1-2,35-38). This is known spiritually as the immersion (baptism) into the cloud (1 Corinthians 10:1-2; Hebrews 6:1-2). The cloud was a covering shelter and protection by day, and was a pillar of fire by night. It was warmth, light, and protection.

Spiritual Understanding (Halacha). The cloud was seen as a *chupah*, a wedding canopy. In Daniel 7:13 it is written,

"...the Son of man came with the clouds of heaven...." This is also mentioned in Revelation 1:7-8 and Jude 14. Here we see that the clouds are the believers in Messiah or the righteous (*tzaddikim*). The same can be seen in Hebrews 12:1. Also look at Isaiah (*Yeshayahu*) 60:8 and Acts 1:9-12.

Remember, the cloud does not only refer to the believers in the Messiah, but was also seen as a *chupah*, a wedding canopy. In Isaiah (*Yeshayahu*) 4:2, it speaks of the branch of the L-rd. This is defined in Isaiah (*Yeshayahu*) 11:1 as being *Yeshua*. In Isaiah (*Yeshayahu*) 11:1, the Hebrew word *netser* is a masculine form translated as "branch." In Isaiah (*Yeshayahu*) 4:2, the Hebrew word translated as branch is *tzemach*, which is neuter. We can see from this that a marriage is being performed. This is very clear in Jeremiah (*Yermiyahu*) 23:5-6; 33:15-16.

In Isaiah (*Yeshayahu*) 4:5 it is written, "...for upon all the glory shall be a defence [*chupah*, or wedding canopy]." Isaiah (*Yeshayahu*) 4:2-6 connects the branch in verse 23 with the cloud in verses 5-6 and the duty that is performed in the wilderness. Isaiah is talking how this would happen during the Messianic Kingdom (Isaiah [*Yeshayahu*] 2:2-4; 4:2-3). Those written among the living in Jerusalem (*Yerushalayim*) actually have their names written in the Lamb's Book of Life (Revelation 3:5; 13:8; 20:12,15; 21:27; Philippians 4:3; Daniel 12:1; Psalm [*Tehillim*] 69:28; Exodus [*Shemot*] 32:31-33).

In Isaiah (*Yeshayahu*) 4:2, it speaks of the fruit of the earth and those who have escaped. *Sukkot* (Tabernacles) is known as the festival of ingathering and the fruit harvest. In Revelation 7:9-17, we can see those who have come through the great tribulation period (the birthpangs of the Messiah or *Chevlai shel Mashiach*) and who became believers in the Messiah during that time (Revelation 7:14). In Revelation 7:15, they "dwell" with them.

This Greek word, *sk'enos*, means "tabernacle, booth, shelter, or covering." This also appears in Revelation 21:3. This same word, *sk'enos*, which means "tabernacle" or "booth" in Greek, is used to speak of *Yeshua* during His first coming (John [*Yochanan*] 1:14). Notice the protection provided in Revelation 7:16, corresponding to Isaiah (*Yeshayahu*) 4:5-6, and the fountain of living waters in Revelation 7:17 and 21:4. In Isaiah (*Yeshayahu*) 4:3, it is written "And it shall come to pass, that he that is left in Zion, and he that remaineth in Jerusalem, shall be called holy..." (also see Zechariah 14:4,6-9,16-17,20-21). Those who are called "holiness unto the Lord" in Zechariah 14:20 are the same people in Isaiah 4:3 who are called holy.

The clouds in the wilderness are called "the clouds of glory" and the wilderness experience is a picture of the future Messianic age, the Millennium. The *sukkah* was built to teach and understand the thousand-year millennial reign of the Messiah, the Messianic age, the Millennium, or the *Athid Lavo* in Hebrew eschatology.

Understanding the Meaning of Booths/Tabernacles

The Hebrew word for tabernacle is *sukkah*. It means "a booth, a hut, a covering, a pavilion or tent." The Greek word for tabernacle is *sk'en'e,* which also means "a tent, hut, or habitation." With this in mind, let's look at the context by which the word *tabernacle* is used in the New Covenant (*Brit Hadashah*).

1. *Yeshua* tabernacled (*sukkot*) among us (John [*Yochanan*] 1:14).

2. Peter (*Kefa*) spoke about his body being a tabernacle (2 Peter [*Kefa*] 1:13-14).

3. The apostle Paul (*Rav Sha'ul*) told us that our earthly bodies were earthly houses or tabernacles (2 Corinthians 5:1-5).

4. The tabernacle of Moses (*Moshe*) was a tent of habitation (Acts 7:44; Hebrews 9:2-8).

5. Abraham (*Avraham*), Isaac (*Yitzchak*), and Jacob (*Ya'akov*) lived in tabernacles (tents) (Hebrews 11:8-9).

6. The tabernacle of David was a tent or dwelling place (Acts 15:16; Amos 9:11). This tabernacle was the temple of Solomon (1 Kings [*Melachim*] 5:2-5; 8:1-21).

7. *Yeshua* entered the temple on the Feast of *Sukkot* (Tabernacles) (John [*Yochanan*] 7:2,27-29).

8. The Bible speaks of a heavenly tabernacle (Hebrews 8:1-2; Revelation 13:6; 15:5). This heavenly tabernacle will come to earth (Revelation 21:1-3).

9. *Yeshua* was the true tabernacle of G-d (Hebrews 9:11).[6]

So, the booth or *sukkah* was a temporary dwelling place. Historically, it was to remind the people of their exodus from Egypt (*Mitzrayim*) as described in Leviticus (*Vayikra*) 23:42-43. Prophetically, the sukkah points toward the future to the Messianic age, the Millennium. Spiritually, a *sukkah* is supposed to remind us that we are but strangers and pilgrims on the earth, this being a temporary dwelling place. So the believer in Messiah is but a stranger and pilgrim on this earth (Hebrews 11:8-10,13-16; Genesis [*Bereishit*] 23:3-4; 47:9; 1 Chronicles [*Divery Hayamim*] 29:10,15; Psalm (*Tehillim*) 39:12; 119:19; 1 Peter [*Kefa*] 1:17; 2:11).

To the believer in *Yeshua*, our earthly physical body is only a temporary tabernacle. At the coming of Messiah, we will receive a new and heavenly house, a glorified body (1 Corinthians 15:39-44,51-57; 2 Corinthians 5:6; 1 Thessalonians 4:15-18).

The Festival of Ingathering

Sukkot (Tabernacles) is the fall harvest festival. It begins on the fifteenth of the Hebrew month of Tishrei and concludes on the twenty-second with *Shemini Atzeret/Simchat* Torah, also called the eighth day, the rejoicing in the Torah. *Shemini Atzeret* functions as the conclusion of *Sukkot*, but it is also a separate festival (this will be discussed in the following chapter).

Like the other pilgrimage festivals, *Sukkot* [Tabernacles] has an agricultural element. It marks the time of the harvest, the final ingathering of produce before the oncoming winter. Hence, it is also called *Hag HaAsif*, the festival of Ingathering. As it is written, "You shall celebrate the Festival of Ingathering, at the end of the year, when you gather in your labors out of the field" (Exodus [*Shemot*] 23:16).[7]

Sukkot is the time when the produce of the field, orchard, and vineyard is gathered in. The granaries, threshing floors, and wine and olive presses are full to capacity. Weeks and months of toil and sweat put into the soil have finally been amply rewarded. The farmer feels happy and elated. No wonder *Sukkot* is "The Season of Rejoicing."[8] While all of the three pilgrimages are times of rejoicing, *Sukkot* (Tabernacles) is specifically designated as *Zeman simchatenu*, the season of our rejoicing.[9]

Ushpizin

As part of *Hachnasat Orechim*, the *mitzvah* of hospitality, there is a custom of inviting *ushpizin*, symbolic guests, each day to join (the family) in the *Sukkah*. These honorary guests are Abraham (*Avraham*), Isaac (*Yitzchak*), Jacob (*Ya'akov*), Joseph (*Yosef*), Moses (*Moshe*), Aaron (*Ahrahon*), and David. One is invited each day.[10]

Spiritual Application (Halacha). As stated earlier, *Sukkot* (Tabernacles) is called the Feast of Ingathering. *Yeshua* told us that the harvest represents the end of the age (*olam Hazeh*). This is found in (Matthew [*Mattityahu*] 13:39; Revelation 14:15; Joel [*Yoel*] 3:13). The harvest refers more specifically to people who choose to accept the Messiah *Yeshua* into their hearts and lives (Matthew [*Mattityahu*] 9:35-38; Luke 10:1-2; John [*Yochanan*] 4:35-38; Revelation 14:14-18). G-d is gathering both Jews and non-Jews together to accept the Messiah *Yeshua* into their lives. Most of the people on earth have not accepted *Yeshua* into their lives and are in the valley of decision (Joel [*Yoel*] 3:13-14). What is your decision? Will you accept the Messiah *Yeshua* into your life?

Jeremiah (*Yermiyahu*) sorrowed for a people who were not a part of the harvest in Jeremiah (*Yermiyahu*) 8:18-22. In Jeremiah 8:20 it is written, "The harvest is past, the summer is ended, and we are not saved." To those who do accept the

Messiah, you will experience the *real Sukkot* (Tabernacles) during the Messianic age, the Millennium. Both Jew and non-Jew will live in the Messianic Kingdom. There will also be immortal people such as Abraham, Isaac, Jacob, Joseph, Moses, Aaron, and David. There will be mortal people as well who will live with them. The mortal people who will be there are the people who lived through the seven-year tribulation period, the birthpangs of the Messiah, or the *Chevlai shel Mashiach*, and who accepted *Yeshua* into their hearts and lives. What a joy it will be living with the Messiah during the Messianic era!

The Feast of Dedication

King Solomon (*Shlomo*) dedicated the temple (*Beit HaMikdash*) during *Sukkot* (Tabernacles) (1 Kings 8). Therefore, this festival is also called the Feast of Dedication. It was celebrated after the Babylonian captivity (Ezra 3:1-4).

The Feast of the Nations

Another name for the Feast of *Sukkot* (Tabernacles) is the Feast of the Nations. *Sukkot* (Tabernacles) will be celebrated by all the nations on earth during the Messianic age, the Millennium (Zechariah 14:16-18). The future observance of *Sukkot* by the nations of the world rests upon Israel's election and mission. The universal concern of G-d's plan for the Jewish people reaches back to the covenant with Abraham (*Avraham*). In that agreement, G-d promised in Genesis (*Bereishit*) 12:3, as it is written, "...all families of the earth [shall] be blessed [through his seed]." From Abraham (*Avraham*), G-d would raise up a people, Israel, to be a blessing to the nations.[11] That promise was fulfilled through *Yeshua*, the Messiah, as stated in Galatians 3:8,14,16,29. In fact, the greatest evangelism in the history of the world will be by 144,000 anointed members from the tribes of Israel proclaiming the gospel (*basar*) of the Kingdom of Heaven through *Yeshua HaMashiach* (Revelation 14:1-7).

A fascinating and mysterious pattern emerges from the seemingly endless list of sacrifices found in Numbers (*Bamidbar*) 29:12-35. During the week of *Sukkot* (Tabernacles), 70 bullocks were offered on the altar. The connection of the 70 bulls to the 70 nations is taken from Deuteronomy (*Devarim*) 32:8; Genesis (*Bereishit*) 46:27; and Exodus (*Shemot*) 1:1-5. Once again, the association of the nations of the world to *Sukkot* (Tabernacles) is found in Zechariah 14:16-19.

When Jacob (*Ya'akov*) and his family went to Egypt (*Mitzrayim*), there were 70 people who went, and it was there that they became a nation. The nations of the world are associated with *Sukkot* (Tabernacles) in First Kings (*Melachim*) 8:41-43 when Solomon dedicated the temple (*Beit HaMikdash*) during *Sukkot* (Tabernacles). For this reason, the festival is also called the Feast of the Nations.

Another fascinating thing about the sacrifices during *Sukkot* (Tabernacles) is that when the offerings are grouped or counted, their number always remains divisible by seven. During the week, there are 182 sacrifices (70 bullocks, 14 rams, and 98 lambs; 7 divides into 182 exactly 26 times). Add to this the meal offerings, 336 tenths of ephahs of flour (48 x 7) (Numbers [*Bamidbar*] 29:12-40). It is no coincidence that this seven-day holiday, which takes place at the height of the seventh month, had the perfect number, seven, imprinted on its sacrifices.

Sukkot is a picture of the Messianic Kingdom (thousand-year reign of the Messiah) as the joy, and the number seven was connected to the sabbath, which was also seen as a picture of the Messianic Kingdom. The sabbath (*shabbat*) falls on the seventh day of the week.

Although G-d is concerned for the universal redemption of the nations, those nations who do not turn to G-d will be judged. Either they will not receive rain (Zechariah 14:1-9, 16-18), or rain will destroy them and be a curse upon them (Ezekiel [*Yechezekel*] 38:22-23). This is why the traditional Bible reading for the second day of *Sukkot* is Zechariah 14 and Ezekiel 38:14 to 39:16.

The Four Species (*Arba Minim*)

In Leviticus (*Vayikra*) 23:40, it is written, "On the first day you shall take the product of goodly trees, branches of palm trees, boughs of leafy trees, and willows of the brook, and you shall rejoice before the L-rd your G-d seven days."[12]

The four species are also called the *Lulav and Etrog* (the palm branches and citron). So, "the product of goodly trees" is interpreted by the rabbis to refer specifically to an *etrog* (citron), and the branches, "boughs of leafy trees," and "willows of the brook" have been interpreted as a *lulav* (palm branch), *hadasim* (myrtle), and *aravot* (willows), respectively.[13]

Whether or not *Sukkot* (Tabernacles) was regularly celebrated during the period of the first temple (*Beit HaMikdash*) is not clear. After the return from Babylon, Nehemiah (*Nechemiah*) wrote that from the days of Joshua's (*Yehoshua*) crossing into the land of Israel until his own day, the children of Israel had not built the huts of *Sukkot* (Nehemiah [*Nechemiah*] 8:17). But from Nehemiah's day forward, the festival was celebrated during the time of the second temple (*Beit HaMikdash*). Each celebrant brought an *etrog* or *citron*, the yellow citrus fruit that is about the same size as a lemon, but sweeter and spicier to serve as the "fruit of goodly trees" that is mentioned in Leviticus (*Vayikra*) 23:40. Each brought as well the branches of a palm, of a myrtle, and of a willow. The three branches were held in the right hand and the *etrog* on the left, and they were brought together to be waved east, south, west, north, up, and down. Since the palm branch, or *lulav*, was the stiffest and the most prominent element of the four species, the whole ceremony was called the waving of the *lulav*.[14]

The four plants are also used during the *Sukkot* holiday in making a *hakafa* (circuit) around the congregation standing in the synagogue. The cantor leads the procession, and each man who has a *lulav* and *etrog* follows behind him. During the procession, the cantor recites the Hoshanah prayers, asking for blessings on the land and fruit of Israel.[15]

Spiritual Application (Halacha). As part of the Feast of Ingathering, palm branches, myrtle branches, and willow branches are collected and held in the right hand (Leviticus [*Vayikra*] 23:40). A fourth entity, the *etrog*, representing the Gentiles or non-Jewish believers, is also gathered. These four species are used in a ceremony for *Sukkot* (Tabernacles). At the start of the ceremony, the *etrog* is upside down. The spiritual meaning is, before we came to G-d, we were in a state of being upside down. Through the ceremony, it is turned right side up and joined to the other three. This represents a marriage that is taking place. After we are turned right side up and turn to G-d, we later are joined to Him in marriage.

In Deuteronomy (*Devarim*) 16:14, the *etrog* also represents the stranger. The stranger is the Gentile who has joined himself to Israel (Ephesians 2:11-13). This is symbolic of the great congregation of non-Jewish believers in the Messiah *Yeshua*.

The Celebration of Water Pouring
(*Simchat Beit HaShoevah*)

Simchat Beit HaShoevah, the rejoicing in the house of the water pouring, is a ceremony included in the temple (*Beit HaMikdash*) services not mentioned in the Torah, but given in the Mishnah (Succah 5). The water pouring became a focus of the joy that the Torah commands for *Sukkot*. On no other festival were the people commanded to be joyful, and as a result *Sukkot* (Tabernacles) became known as "the season of our joy," just as Passover (*Pesach*) is "the season of our freedom" and *Shavout* (Pentecost) is "the season of the giving of the Torah."[16]

It is written in the Mishnah that the ritual became elaborated into a colorful and joyous, even riotous, celebration called *Simchat Beit HaShoevah*, "the rejoicing at the house of the water-drawing." This ceremony took place every day except for the first festival day of *Sukkot*. The Talmud (in Sukkah 51a-b) describes this ceremony in detail, including a portrait of venerable sages juggling lighted torches and performing somersaults as part of the celebration. The Talmud states, "He who has not seen the rejoicing at the place of the water-drawing has never seen rejoicing in his life."[17] So, the water pouring ceremony became the occasion for an out-pouring of intense joy.[18]

The Daily *Sukkot* Ceremony

Each day out of the temple (*Beit HaMikdash*), there was a special ceremony. The priests were divided into three divisions. The first division were the priests on duty for that festival. They would slay the sacrifices found in Numbers (*Bamidbar*) 29. At this time, a second group of priests went out the eastern gate of the temple (*Beit HaMikdash*) and went to the *Motzah* Valley, where the ashes were dumped at the beginning of the sabbath. There they would cut willows. The willows had to be 25 feet in length. After this, they would form a line with all the priests holding a willow. About 25 or 30 feet behind this row of priests, allowing room for the willows, would be another row of priests with willows. So, there would be row after row of the willows.

The whole road back to the temple (*Beit HaMikdash*) was lined with pilgrims as they went to Jerusalem (*Yerushalayim*) to celebrate the festival as they were commanded by G-d to do. *Sukkot* (Tabernacles), along with *Shavuot* (Pentecost), and Passover (*Pesach*), were known as the pilgrimage festivals (Deuteronomy 16:16).

There would be a signal and the priests would step out with their left foot, and then step to the right, swinging the willows back and forth. Meanwhile, a third group of priests, headed by the high priest (*Cohen HaGadol*), went out the gate known as the Water Gate. They had gone to the pool known as "Siloam" (John [*Yochanan*] 9:7,11), which means "gently flowing waters." There the high priest had a golden vase and drew the water known as the living water (*mayim hayim*) and held it in the vase. His assistant held a silver vase containing wine. Just as the priests in the valley of *Motzah* began to march toward Jerusalem (*Yerushalayim*), so did the priests in Siloam. As they marched toward the city of Jerusalem (*Yerushalayim*), the willows made a swishing sound in the wind as they approached the city. The word *wind* in Hebrew is *Ruach*. The word *spirit* in Hebrew is also *Ruach*. Therefore, this ceremony was symbolic or representative of the Holy Spirit (*Ruach HaKodesh*) of G-d coming upon the city of Jerusalem (*Yerushalayim*).

As each of the party reached their respective gates, a trumpet (*shofar*) was blown. Then one man would stand up and play the flute (the flute represents the Messiah). The flute player is called "the pierced one." The flute is pierced, and *Yeshua* was pierced during the crucifixion (Psalm [*Tehillim*] 22:16; Zechariah 12:10; John [*Yochanan*] 19:34-37; Revelation 1:7).

The flute player led the procession. The pierced one blows the call for the wind and the water to enter the temple. The priests from *Motzah* swishing the willows come into the temple (*Beit HaMikdash*) and circle the altar seven times. The priests that were slaying the sacrifices are now ascending the altar, and they begin to lay the sacrifices on the fires. The high priest and his assistant ascend the altar and all the people of Israel are gathered into the courts around there. The people start singing the song *Mayim*, saying, "With joy we will draw water out of the well of salvation [*Yeshua*]" (Isaiah [*Yeshayahu*] 12:3; Mishnah, Sukkah 5:1). The high priest takes his vase and pours its contents on one of the corners of the altar where the horns are. There are two bowls built into the altar. Each bowl has a hole in it. The water and the wine are poured out over the altar as the priests who had the willow start laying the willows against the altar, making a *sukkah* (a picture of G-d's covering).[19]

Messianic Understanding. In this, we have a picture of *Yeshua* as He was on the tree. He was on the altar (tree) when His heart was pierced (John [*Yochanan*] 19:34), then the water and the blood separated and they were poured out. G-d through *Yeshua* was providing a covering (*sukkah*) for all those who would believe in Him.

Wine is representative of marriage, blood, covenant, joy, and the Messiah in Scripture. The priests took the willows to the altar and set them upright on the side of the altar, forming a wedding canopy or *chupah*. The high priest will take his golden vessel and pour out the water on the altar. The assistant will pour out his silver vessel of wine on the altar. When *Yeshua* was crucified on the tree (a type of altar), His side was pierced and out of His heart poured water and blood (John [*Yochanan*] 19:34). *Yeshua* said that He was the living water being poured out during this ceremony (John [*Yochanan*] 7:2,37-38).

Spiritual Application (Halacha). During the time of *Yeshua*, the Feast of *Sukkot* set a magnificent stage for the preaching of the Messiah. Rain is essential to the growing of crops and Israel, an arid land, prizes rain greatly as a blessing from G-d.[20]

Rain was a prominent feature in the celebration of the Feast of *Sukkot*. The ceremony of the water drawing held a significance much deeper than its agricultural implications. The rain represented the Holy Spirit (*Ruach HaKodesh*) and the water drawing pointed to that day when, according to the prophet Joel [*Yoel*], G-d would rain His Spirit upon (all flesh) (Joel [*Yoel*] 2:28-29). The connection of water to this verse is G-d pouring out His Spirit. In the Talmud we read, "Why is the name of it called the drawing out of water? Because of the pouring out of the Holy Spirit, according to what is said, 'With joy shall ye draw out of the wells of salvation' " (Isaiah [*Yeshayahu*] 12:3).[21]

Sukkot was given by G-d to teach us of the Messianic era, the Millennium, when the earth will experience the greatest outpouring of G-d's Spirit.

Hoshana Rabbah (The Great Salvation)

Hoshana Rabbah (literally, the great hosanna or the numerous hosannas) is the seventh day of *Sukkot* (Tabernacles). *Hoshana Rabbah* should have been a full festival day, but is not because of *Shemini Atzeret*, which follows it. However, it has some special rituals and customs that make the day more like a full festival day than any of the intermediate days. The most important of these (ceremonies) are:

1. The circling of the altar seven times instead of once while carrying the four species and reciting the *hoshana* prayers.
2. The beating of the willows.[22]

Messianic Understanding. In John (*Yochanan*) 7:37-38, *Yeshua* said, "If any man thirst, let him come unto Me, and drink. He that believeth on Me, as the scripture hath said, out of his belly shall flow rivers of living water."

At this season of *Sukkot*, Isaiah (*Yeshayahu*) 12:3 was often quoted, as it is written, "Therefore with joy shall ye draw water out of the wells of salvation." *Yeshua* in Hebrew means "salvation."

The drama of the water drawing ceremony took on a new dimension of meaning when *Yeshua* attended the Feast of *Sukkot* (Tabernacles). On the seventh day of the feast, *Hoshana Rabbah*, which literally means "the great hosanna, the great salvation," the festival activities were different from those of each of the six previous days when the priests circled the altar in a procession, singing Psalm (*Tehillim*) 118:25. On the seventh day of the feast, the people circled the altar seven times. That is why the day is called *Hoshanah Rabbah*, as the cry, "Save now!" was repeated seven times. *Yeshua's* statement in John (*Yochanan*) 7:37-39 was said on *Hoshana Rabbah*.

Spiritual Application (Halacha). Spiritually speaking, in the Bible, there is a link between water and the outpouring of the Holy Spirit (*Ruach HaKodesh*). *Yeshua* told the woman at the well to drink of living water (John [*Yochanan*] 4:7-14; 6:35; Matthew [*Mattityahu*] 5:6). This relationship between water and the outpouring of the Holy Spirit (*Ruach Ha-Kodesh*) is contained in the symbolism of pouring out water. Isaiah (*Yeshayahu*) 44:3 links the pouring out of water with the pouring out of G-d's Spirit. Isaiah (*Yeshayahu*) parallels the thirsty land and links water with the Holy Spirit. The link can also be seen in Joel (*Yoel*) 2:23,28; Acts 2:1-4,14-17; and Ezekiel (*Yechezekel*) 39:22,27-29. Zechariah 14:8 speaks of living waters. Isaiah (*Yeshayahu*) 12:2-3 speaks of drawing water out of the wells of salvation. Water and the Spirit are connected in Psalm (*Tehillim*) 42:1-4; Zechariah 13:1; and Revelation 7:17. It can also be seen in Ezekiel (*Yechezekel*) 36:24-27.

Yeshua was trying to communicate this to Nicodemus (*Nakdimon*) in John (*Yochanan*) 3:1-6. He also was teaching this during the Feast of *Sukkot* (Tabernacles) in John (*Yochanan*) 4:14, which concluded with His statements in John 7:37-39. At the ceremony of the water drawing, the people's attention was focused on the pool of Siloam.[23] It was here that *Yeshua* healed a man who had been blind from birth (John [*Yochanan*] 9:1-7). Notice again the statement in John 9:5. This is the last day of the feast (*Hoshana Rabbah*) (John 9:14; Leviticus [*Vayikra*] 23:34-36).

The Festival of Lights (The Light of the Temple)

Another ceremony of the Feast of *Sukkot* (Tabernacles) was the illumination of the temple (*Beit HaMikdash*). According to the Mishnah, at the end of the first day of the Feast of *Sukkot* (Tabernacles), the priests and the Levites went down to the court of the women. Four enormous golden candlesticks were set up on the court (50 cubits high) with four golden bowls placed upon them and four ladders resting against each candlestick. Four youths of priestly descent stood at the top of the ladders holding jars containing about 7.5 gallons of pure oil, which they poured for each bowl (Mishnah, Sukkah 5:2). The priests and Levites used their own worn-out liturgical clothing for wicks. The light emanating from the four candelabras was so bright that the Mishnah says in Sukkah 5:3 that there was no courtyard in

Jerusalem [*Yerushalayim*] that was not lit up with the light of the libation water-well ceremony (*Beit Hashoevah*).

The mood was festive. Pious men, members of the San Hedrin, and heads of different religious schools would dance well into the night, holding bright torches and singing psalms of praise to G-d. Jerusalem (*Yerushalayim*) glistened like a diamond that night and her light could be seen from afar.[24]

Spiritual Application (Halacha). Spiritually speaking, the light represented the *shekinah* glory that once filled the temple where G-d's presence dwelt in the Holy of Holies (1 Kings 8:10-11; Ezekiel 43:5). During this time, the temple (*Beit HaMikdash*) was thought of as "the light of the world." In the brilliance of this gloriously lit temple, *Yeshua* cried in John (*Yochanan*) 8:12 that He was "the light of the world."[25]

In addition, during this festival of *Sukkot* (Tabernacles) and this time, in the court of the women of the temple between the four posts of light, the accusers brought to *Yeshua* the woman caught in the act of adultery (John [*Yochanan*] 8:1-11). *Yeshua* forgave the woman and proceeded to write a message on the ground (John [*Yochanan*] 8:5-9). What did *Yeshua* write? The answer is in Jeremiah 17:13. In these things, we can see that *Yeshua* taught the people the messages of the festivals during the festivals.

Israel: A Light (Witness) to the Nations

Israel was chosen to be G-d's light to the world (Deuteronomy [*Devarim*] 7:6-8). The mission that G-d chose for Israel was one of service to G-d. The reason is very simple. G-d wanted a people out of the world whom He could use and work through to show His glory to the world. That is why He chose Israel and that is what every follower of the Messiah is chosen to be. In doing so, G-d could reveal His redemptive plan to the whole world so the world could see that G-d and His Messiah *Yeshua* are light (John 1:1-4; 1 John 1:5). Israel was to be a witness (light) to the world. This can be seen in the following Scriptures: Isaiah (*Yeshayahu*) 43:1,10,12,14; Luke 24:44-49; and Acts 1:1-8. Israel's mission was to proclaim to the world that the G-d of Israel is the only true G-d and there is no other Savior but He (Acts 4:10,12).

Israel as a corporate nation failed in her mission to be a witness to the world. Not only were the people disobedient to the commandment of G-d, but they also did not become a light to the world. On the contrary, the world as a corporate people have always hated the nation of Israel.

As individual members who believed and followed after G-d, the Hebrew people were faithful to their task. We only need to consider the faithfulness of Abraham, Isaac, Jacob, Moses, the prophets, and the kings such as David and Solomon. In fact, consider the very Bible which you are able to read today; it was written by faithful Israelite servants of G-d led by the Holy Spirit (*Ruach HaKodesh*) of G-d. Most of all, the greatest light and witness the world has ever known was Jewish. His name is *Yeshua*, the Messiah! Because Israel birthed the Messiah, they, in essence, have been a blessing to all nations through Him (Genesis [*Bereishit*] 12:3; Galatians 3:8,14,16,29).

Although Israel corporately failed in her mission, this is not a permanent failure. It is a temporary setback to her

destiny of being a blessing to all nations, which will be accomplished during the thousand-year reign of the Messiah
known as the Messianic Kingdom or the Messianic age. Israel still remains G-d's chosen people (Romans 11:25-29),
and still has a role to play in the future of the world (Romans
11:12,15). The prophet Isaiah (*Yeshayahu*) spoke of a future
time when Israel would be used by G-d to bring the message
of Messiah to the nations, for the nation of Israel will have a
central part in the thousand-year reign of the Messiah (Isaiah
[*Yeshayahu*] 62:1-5). Israel will be a blessing to all nations at
this time (Malachi 3:12; Ezekiel [*Yechezekel*] 34:23-30;
Zechariah 8:11-15; Isaiah [*Yeshayahu*] 19:23-25). Jerusalem
(*Yerushalayim*) will be the spiritual focal point of the world
and this time will be Israel's "Golden Age," during the Messianic era, because the King of Jerusalem, the Prince of
Peace, will reign in Jerusalem (*Yerushalayim*) (Isaiah
[*Yeshayahu*] 2:2-4; 52:9-10; 62:7-8, Micah [*Michah*] 4:1-3;
Psalm [*Tehillim*] 102:18-21; 125:1-2; 137:5-6). The day is
coming when a restored and renewed Israel will once again
be a light to the nations, for the destiny of Israel is linked to
the destiny of the world!

The Birth of *Yeshua* During *Sukkot*

The Scriptures seem to indicate to us that *Yeshua* was
born during the festival season of *Sukkot* (Tabernacles). In
fact, I believe that He was born on the Feast of *Sukkot* (which
is Tishrei 15 on the biblical calendar, and is analogous to our
September/October). With this in mind, let's look for some
evidence of this in the Bible.

In Luke 1:5, Zachariah (*Z'kharyah*) is a priest (*cohen*) of
the division of Abijah (*Avijah*). What does this mean? Israel

was divided into 24 districts at the time of *Yeshua*. Each of these districts sent two representatives to officiate at the temple during the weeks of the year. In First Chronicles (*Divery Hayamim*) 24, the first division of the priests would serve in the first week of the year, which would be both in the month of Nisan and the month of Tishrei since both months begin the new year. As we saw earlier in this book, Nisan is the first month in the religious calendar set up by G-d in Exodus (*Shemot*) 12:2 and Tishrei is the first month of the year according to the civil calendar.

During the third week in the month of Nisan, the priests from all 24 districts would come to the temple to help during the week of Passover (*Pesach*). This would also be the case for the festival of Pentecost (*Shavuot*) and for the festival of *Sukkot* (Tabernacles) when all males were required to go to Jerusalem (*Yerushalayim*) as specified by G-d in Deuteronomy (*Devarim*) 16:16. In First Chronicles 24:10, we see that *abijah* was the eighth division or course of priests. The course of *abijah* would minister during the tenth week of the year. Remember, the weeks of Passover and *Shavuot* would not be counted because all the priests were required to go to Jerusalem then.

In Luke 1:9-10, we see that Zacharias is burning incense. This is done in the room of the temple known as the Holy Place. As the incense (which represents the prayers of G-d's people [Psalm (*Tehillim*) 141:2; Revelation 8:3-4]) is being burned by the priests in the temple, 18 special prayers are prayed. These 18 prayers would be prayed every day in the temple. One of these prayers is that Elijah (*Eliyahu*) would come. This is important because it was understood by the people, as G-d established, that Elijah (*Eliyahu*) would precede the coming of the Messiah as stated in Malachi 4:5. These 18 special prayers would be prayed twice a day, once in the morning and once in the afternoon. In Luke 1:11-13, the angel appeared on the right side of the altar and told Zacharias that his prayer was heard and John (*Yochanan*) the Immerser (Baptist) would be born. John (*Yochanan*) the Immerser (Baptist) was not literally Elijah (*Eliyahu*), but was of the spirit of power of Elijah (Luke 1:17).

Allowing two weeks for the laws of separation that G-d commanded in Leviticus (*Vayikra*) 12:5; 15:19,24-25 after going back to the house (Luke 1:23) and then going forward nine months (Sivan [tenth week] + 2 weeks + 9 months) puts the birth of John (*Yochanan*) during the festival of Passover (*Pesach*). This is an extremely important point because during the service for Passover, which is called the Passover Seder, the people are instructed by G-d to go to the door during one part of the service and look for Elijah (*Eliyahu*) while the Passover meal is eaten. The cup is called the cup of Elijah. The understanding of Elijah preceding the coming of the Messiah was the basis for the question in Matthew (*Mattityahu*) 17:10-13.

In Luke 1:26 during the sixth month of Elisabeth's (*Elisheva*) pregnancy, the angel Gabriel appeared to Mary (*Miryam*). This should have been around the twenty-fifth of Kislev, otherwise known as *Chanukah*. During the time of the first century, *Chanukah* was known as the second *Sukkot*. During the time of *Chanukah*, all of the *Sukkot* prayers are prayed once again. Mary's (*Miryam*) dialogue with the angel Gabriel is found in the *Sukkot* liturgy today. If you calculate from the twenty-fifth of Kislev and add eight days for the festival of *Chanukah* plus nine months for Mary's (*Miryam*) pregnancy, this will bring you around the time of the festival of *Sukkot*, or Tishrei 15. On Tishrei 22, known as *Shemini Atzeret* or the eighth day, *Yeshua* was circumcised (Luke 2:22-23; Leviticus [*Vayikra*] 12:1-3).[26]

Other Evidences of *Yeshua's* Birth During *Sukkot*

As we have stated earlier in this chapter, the Feast of *Sukkot* (Tabernacles) is called "the season of our joy" and "the feast of the nations." With this in mind, in Luke 2:10 it is written, "And the angel said unto them, Fear not: for, behold, I bring you good tidings [*basar* in Hebrew; otherwise known as the gospel] of great joy [*Sukkot* is called the 'season of our joy'], which shall be to all people [*Sukkot* is called 'the feast of the nations']." So, we can see from this that the terminology the angel used to announce the birth of *Yeshua* were themes and messages associated with the Feast of *Sukkot* (Tabernacles).

In Luke 2:12, the babe (*Yeshua*) was wrapped in swaddling cloths and lying in a manger. The swaddling cloths were also used as wicks to light the 16 vats of oil within the court of the women during the festival of *Sukkot*. So, swaddling cloths are associated with the festival of *Sukkot*.

Notice also in Luke 2:12 that the baby *Yeshua* was laid in a manger. The word *manger* is the Greek word *phatn'e*. It is the same word translated as "stall" in Luke 13:15. By seeing how the word is used in Luke 13:15, we can see that the Greek word *phatn'e* means a place for hitching cattle. The Hebrew word for stall is *marbek*, which can be found in

Amos 6:4 and Malachi 4:2. In Genesis (*Bereishit*) 33:17 it is written that Jacob journeyed to *Sukkoth* and made booths (the word *booth* in this passage is the Hebrew word *sukkah*; the plural is *sukkot*) for his cattle. So we can see from these passages how the word *booth* (*sukkah* or *sukkot*) was used by Jacob (*Ya'akov*) for his cattle in Genesis 33:17, and how the Greek word for manger or "stall," *phatn'e*, was also used to refer to hitching cattle in Luke 13:15. *Phatn'e* is the same word translated as "manger" in Luke 2:12, where *Yeshua* was laid at the time of His birth.

During the Feast of *Sukkot* (Tabernacles), G-d required that all male Israelites come to Jerusalem (*Yerushalayim*) (Deuteronomy [*Devarim*] 16:16). For this reason, the city would be overcrowded with people and would explain why Mary (*Miryam*) and Joseph (*Yosef*) could not find lodging in and around Jerusalem (*Yerushalayim*) (Luke 2:7). Bethlehem, the place where *Yeshua* was born, is only about four miles from Jerusalem.

The last evidence I will give for the birth of *Yeshua* during *Sukkot* according to the Scriptures is in Matthew (*Mattityahu*) 2:1. There we see that wise men come from the East to visit *Yeshua*. The land of the East is Babylon, where the largest Jewish population was at the time of the birth of *Yeshua*. These Jews were descendants from the captivity when King Nebuchadnezzar defeated Israel and took the Jews to Babylon to serve him. Babylon is referred to as the land of the East in Genesis (*Bereishit*) 29:1 and Judges (*Shoftim*) 6:3. The wise men in Matthew (*Mattityahu*) 2:1 were rabbis. The rabbis, also called sages, are known in

Hebrew as *chakamim*, which means wise men. The word in Matthew (*Mattityahu*) 2:1 in Greek is *magos*, which is translated into English as "Magi." *Magos* in Greek is the Hebrew word *ravmag*. *Ravmag* comes from the Hebrew word *rav*, which means "rabbi." It should also be noted that the Greek word *magos* can also mean scientist, counselor, scholar, or teacher. The rabbis were scholars or teachers of the Jewish law. *Yeshua* was referred to as "Rabbi," or "Teacher" in John (*Yochanan*) 1:38,47,49; 3:2. So, we can see that the wise men were Jewish rabbis coming from Babylon to witness the birth of *Yeshua*.

A question we can ask ourselves is, "What made the rabbis make the journey from Babylon to Bethlehem to witness the birth of *Yeshua*?" The answer is given in Matthew (*Mattityahu*) 2:2, as it is written, "...we have seen His *star* in the east...."

One of the requirements during the time of *Sukkot* was to build an outside temporary shelter and live in it during this festival season. This shelter is called a booth, or *sukkah*. The *sukkah* had to be built with an opening in the roof so the people could see the stars in heaven. This is another reason for why the rabbis would be looking for, and thus seeing, the star in the sky when it appeared. In addition, there was a prophecy in Numbers (*Bamidbar*), as it is written, "...a *star* shall come forth from Jacob..." (Numbers [*Bamidbar*] 24:17 NAS). King Herod inquired about where the Messiah would be born in Matthew (*Mattityahu*) 2:4. He was told in Bethlehem (Matthew [*Mattityahu*] 2:5-6), based upon the prophecy in Micah 5:2. In Matthew 2:10 it is written, "When they saw the star, they rejoiced with exceeding great joy." Once again, remember that *Sukkot* is called "the season of our joy." In Matthew 2:2, the rabbis saw the star from the East. Salvation was seen by the Jewish people as coming from the East. *Yeshua* descended from the tribe of Judah (Revelation 5:5). The tribe of Judah was positioned on the east side of the tabernacle of Moses (*Moshe*) in the wilderness. Finally, in Luke 2:32, *Yeshua* is called a light to the Gentiles. Once again, *Sukkot* is called "the festival of lights" and "the festival of all nations."[27]

Therefore, studying and understanding the festival of *Sukkot* and the themes and messages that G-d desired to be conveyed during this festival enables us to read the Bible in a new light; it enables us to understand that *Yeshua* was born during the season of *Sukkot* and that He is the Star we are all called to see with our (spiritual) eyes!

Spiritual Significance of the Feast of *Sukkot*

One of the most outstanding truths of the Feast of *Sukkot* (Tabernacles) involves the seasonal rains in Israel. The prophet Joel (*Yoel*) tells us that the former and latter rain would come in the first month (Joel [*Yoel*] 2:23). This is because Passover (*Pesach*) is the first month in the religious or sacred calendar, and *Sukkot* (Tabernacles) is the first month in the civil calendar. So Israel has two first months in the same year because of the special calendar that G-d set up in Exodus (*Shemot*) 12:2.

Hosea (*Hoshea*) 6:3 tells us that the coming of the Messiah will be as the former and latter rain on the earth. We just saw in the previous section that *Yeshua* came to earth (was born) during the festival of *Sukkot* (Tabernacles), the first month of the civil calendar, and died at His first coming during the first month (Nisan) on the sacred calendar. His second coming will also be in the first month of the civil calendar, Tishrei. *Yeshua* will return to earth during the fall of the year.

G-d promised Israel that upon their obedience to the covenant He made with them at Mount Sinai (Exodus [*Shemot*] 34:10; Deuteronomy [*Devarim*] 5:2; 29:12-15), He would give them the rains in their due season (Deuteronomy [*Devarim*] 11:10-17). No rain was a sign of judgment and the curse of G-d on the land as well as on the people (1 Kings [*Melachim*] 8:33-43; 17:1-7; 18:41-46; Proverbs [*Mishlai*] 16:15; Amos 4:6-13; Joel [*Yoel*] 1:10-12). Today, the land of Israel is becoming green once again (Isaiah [*Yeshayahu*] 35:1; Ezekiel [*Yechezekel*] 36:24-38; Joel [*Yoel*] 2:18-27).

The rain is a type of the Holy Spirit (*Ruach HaKodesh*) being poured out upon all flesh (Acts 2:1-8,14-21; Joel [*Yoel*] 2:23,28-29). The Word of G-d (Torah) is likened to the rain (Deuteronomy [*Devarim*] 32:1-3; Isaiah [*Yeshayahu*] 55:8-12; Ephesians 5:26). The Holy Spirit (*Ruach HaKodesh*) is also likened to the rain (Joel [*Yoel*] 2:21-32; Acts 2:1-8, 14-21; James 5:7; John 7:37-39). Rain is associated with righteousness in Hosea (*Hoshea*) 10:12. G-d has made His righteousness available for all who believe on the Messiah (Romans 3:21-22; 5:17).

Yeshua is the rain that came down from Heaven as well as the living water and the fountain of living water spoken of in

John (*Yochanan*) 4:4-6,10-14,20-24; and Revelation 21:6 and 22:1-5,17. *Yeshua* desires that we drink of the water He gives, which results in everlasting life (John 4:14) that we might be filled (Matthew 5:6).

Rain also speaks of revival, restoration, and returning to G-d (*Teshuvah*) and trusting (*emunah*) in Him. Just as the rain came after Elijah prayed seven times for it (1 Kings [*Melachim*] 18:41-46), the great rain or outpouring of G-d's Holy Spirit will come when the believers in the Messiah will earnestly pray to G-d that it be done. G-d has already declared that He would pour out His Holy Spirit during the seventh month, which is a spiritual picture of the end of the age (*olam Hazeh*). So far, we have for the most part seen only showers of blessing (Ezekiel [*Yechezekel*] 34:26). The greatest outpouring of G-d's Spirit is yet to come. The feast of *Sukkot* (Tabernacles) and the rain speaks of a mighty outpouring of the Holy Spirit of G-d, a universal outpouring of His Spirit. This outpouring will be accompanied by signs and wonders and manifestations of the gift of the Holy Spirit (*Ruach HaKodesh*) as well as a revelation and illumination of the Word of G-d beyond all that has ever been seen in the history of the congregation of believers (*kehilat*) in the Messiah. This outpouring will touch every nation, both Jew and non-Jew. The believer in the Messiah who is living at the time of the latter rain is called to seek the L-rd and ask Him to send rain on the people of the earth (Zechariah 10:1; Psalm [*Tehillim*] 46:4; 65:9-10; Jeremiah [*Yermiyahu*] 5:23-24; 31:10-14).

The fullness of this feast in the seventh month will be experienced at the coming of the Messiah when He will rule and reign on the earth during the Messianic age, the Millennium, called the *Athid Lavo* in Hebrew eschatology. This time will be a time of joy for all believers in the Messiah *Yeshua* and will be the age of Israel's glory.

Chapter 10

Shemini Atzeret
and *Simchat Torah*

Immediately following the last day of *Sukkot*, *Hoshana Rabbah*, is *Shemini Atzeret* (the eighth day of assembly). *Shemini Atzeret* along with *Simchat Torah* are celebrated together on Tishrei 22 and 23. As it is written, "On the eighth day you shall hold a solemn gathering (*Atzeret*); you shall not work at your occupations" (Numbers [*Bamidbar*] 29:35).[1] The rabbis interpreted this verse to mean that G-d asks all who made a pilgrimage for *Sukkot* to tarry (*atzeret*, which comes from the Hebrew root word meaning "to hold back") with Him one additional day. From this, the rabbis concluded that *Shemini Atzeret* is an independent festival.[2]

To understand *Shemini Atzeret* and *Simchat Torah*, we must review a few things. First, the seven days of Passover (*Pesach*) are followed by a 49-day period of counting the *omer*, which climaxes with the fiftieth day of Pentecost (*Shavuot*). Thus, the liberation of Passover (*Pesach*) is linked with the revelation and giving of the Torah at Mount Sinai, known as *Shavuot* (Pentecost).[3] If we look at the festival cycle, *Shemini Atzeret* is analogous to *Shavuot*, which is understood to be the conclusion or *atzeret* to Passover (*Pesach*). Just like *Shavuot*, a one-day festival, is the conclusion to *Pesach*, a seven-day festival, so *Shemini Atzeret*, a one-day festival, is the conclusion to *Sukkot*, a seven-day festival.[4]

Therefore, we see that *Shemini Atzeret* is the eighth day—that is the day after "seven." Seven, being a perfect number in the Bible, signifies a complete unit of time as each week ends with the seventh day called the *Shabbat* (Sabbath). Thus, the eighth day is the day after time. It is the end of both kinds of time. It is thus not just the promise of redemption, but the actual moment of it. G-d said, "Remain with Me (*atzeret*) an extra day," a time beyond time.[5]

Simchat Torah: Rejoicing in the Torah

At last comes the most joyous day of all, the day of *Simchat Torah*, rejoicing in the Torah.[6] *Simchat Torah* is celebrated on the twenty-third of Tishrei, or the day following *Shemini Atzeret*.[7] Once again, it should be noted that the Hebrew word *Torah* means "teaching [or instruction]," for it teaches us our way of life, the kind of life G-d wants us to lead.[8] The Torah is the foundation for understanding the entire Bible.

The Cyclical Reading of the Torah

Until the early Middle Ages, there was more than one cycle with regard to the reading of the Torah. In fact, the most widespread cycle was the triennial one, in which the reading of the Torah took three years and ended before Passover (*Pesach*).[9]

In modern times, the annual reading cycle became predominant. Therefore, *Simchat Torah* became the end of the reading cycle and thus its own festival day. As just stated, the Torah reading cycle is concluded on *Simchat Torah*. However, at this time, it is immediately started again from the beginning. This shows that there is no end to the Torah, and that it must be read and studied constantly, over and over again. The Torah, like G-d Himself who gave it, is everlasting (Matthew [*Mattityahu*] 5:17-18).

Simchat Torah celebrates a Torah of joy, a Torah without restrictions or a sense of burden.[10]

Yeshua and *Shemini Atzeret* and *Simchat Torah*

Tishrei 22, *Shemini Atzeret*, and Tishrei 23, *Simchat Torah*, in ancient times were considered one long day and celebrated on Tishrei 22. *Simchat Torah* is a celebration of rejoicing in the Torah.

As it is written in John (*Yochanan*) 7:37, "In the last day, that great day of the feast [of *Sukkot*]...." This day would be known as *Hoshana Rabbah*, or Tishrei 21. In John (*Yochanan*) 8:1-2, it is written, "Jesus went unto the mount of Olives. And early in the morning He came again into the temple, and all the people came unto Him; and He sat down, and taught them." This is the next day after *Hoshana Rabbah*, the day attached to *Sukkot* called *Shemini Atzeret*. Once again, in ancient times that day was also called *Simchat Torah*, the rejoicing in the Torah. So, in John (*Yochanan*) 8:5, we see *Yeshua*, the author of the Torah, is questioned about the Torah on the day referred to as "the rejoicing in the Torah."

The Spiritual Understanding
of *Shemini Atzeret/Simchat Torah*

In Deuteronomy (*Devarim*) 31:9-13, at the Feast of *Sukkot* (Tabernacles), you are to read the Torah. The seventh year is called the year of release (Deuteronomy [*Devarim*] 31:10); all debts are to be forgiven at this time (Exodus [*Shemot*] 21:2; Leviticus [*Vayikra*] 25:1-4; Deuteronomy [*Devarim*] 15:1-12; Jeremiah [*Yermiyahu*] 34:8-22). The seven years are a picture of the 7,000-year plan of G-d (Psalm [*Tehillim*] 90:4; 2 Peter 3:8). The seventh year is the year of release and is a picture of the seventh day or the Messianic age, the Millennium, or the *Athid Lavo*. *Yeshua* referred to this in both Isaiah (*Yeshayahu*) 61:1-3 and Luke 4:16-21. The phrase, "liberty to the captives" in Isaiah (*Yeshayahu*) 61:1, speaks of the year of release. *Yeshua* is saying, in essence, "I am that release. Trust in Me and you will be free."

In the days of *Yeshua*, there was a seven-year cycle of reading the Torah. In years one through three, the people would read from the Torah, the prophets and the writings. In years three through six, they would start over. In year seven, they would read from them all. While reading, the priest would stand on a podium (*bema*) and give the understanding and teaching (Nehemiah 8:1-12). This was done during the Feast of *Sukkot* (Tabernacles) (Nehemiah 8:2,13-14,18).

In the future, we will experience the real *Simchat Torah* during the time G-d judges the believers in the Messiah according to the lives they lived on this earth. At that time, when we hear the truth of the Bible and understand G-d's Word, we will cry when we see how we have failed to keep and follow the Bible and G-d's truths. But G-d will say, "Do not sorrow, for the joy of the L-rd is your strength" (see Nehemiah [*Nechemiah*] 8:9-10). At this time, we will not be going through the rehearsal (*miqra*) of the festival, but we will be experiencing the "season of our joy," the time of the Messianic kingdom on earth. The reading, teaching, and understanding of the Torah will be at its height during the Messianic age, the Millennium. In Isaiah (*Yeshayahu*) 2:1-5 and Micah (*Michah*) 4:1-5, *Yeshua*, the Messiah, the author and teacher of the Torah, will teach all the peoples of the earth the ways of the Torah.

Rain and Dew, *Geshem* and *Tal*: A Prayer for Rain

On the festival of *Shemini Atzeret*, the *Musaf*, the additional service on this day, begins with a special prayer for rain (*geshem*). The reason for these special prayers is understandable enough (if you have lived in the land of Israel). The winter months in the Holy Land are the rain season, and the entire life of the country depends on rain. If the rains come down in their due season and in sufficient quantity, the rich soil will produce abundant crops and fruits; if not, the country is doomed to famine and starvation. During the summer months, there is no rain; it's the dry season. During these rainless months, the earth would have been completely parched, the top soil would have turned into dust and been blown away by the wind, and the land would have turned into barren desert—were it not for the dew that settles on the cool soil during the hours of the night, drenching the ground with the soft moisture which we know as dew and which sparkles in the early rays of the sun like pearls. Thus, the rain in the winter and the dew in the summer are vitally needed to sustain life.[11]

***Spiritual Application* (*Halacha*).** Because this chapter concludes the festivals, we will review the spiritual significance of the festivals to the individual believer in the Messiah and how they relate to his life. Therefore, at this time, we can conclude with the spiritual significance of the fall festivals, especially *Sukkot*, *Shemini Atzeret*, and *Simchat Torah*.

G-d designed the agricultural and weather seasons in Israel to parallel the life of every believer in *Yeshua* who seeks to love Him and serve Him with all his heart. With this in mind, let us examine how this is true.

Every time a person receives *Yeshua* the Messiah as his own Savior, he spiritually experiences Passover (*Pesach*). He is to flee Egypt (*Mitzrayim*; the world's evil system and ways); trust (*emunah*) in the Messiah, the Lamb of G-d; and allow *Yeshua* to be the doorpost of his heart. As believers, we are then to seek to live holy lives before G-d and experience Unleavened Bread (*Hag HaMatzah*). Just as *Yeshua* rose from the dead, we are to consider our former ways dead to us and experience the newness of life in the Messiah. Once we do this, we can be immersed (baptized) in the Holy Spirit (*Ruach HaKodesh*) and have the power of G-d (the anointing) in our lives. Spiritually, we have experienced the spring harvest of Israel in our lives. When we accept *Yeshua* into our hearts and lives, He begins to teach us the Bible and show us how much He loves us, and we begin to grow in the knowledge of Him.

At that time, G-d will begin to take us on a spiritual journey through the wilderness of life. Spiritually, we will begin to experience the dry summer season of Israel. Many things in our lives will not go the way we expect them to or how we trust G-d for them to go. In the process of experiencing life's bitter disappointments and struggles, if we keep our eyes upon G-d, He will take us from Passover (*Pesach*) to *Shavuot* (Pentecost). There He will reveal His ways and His Word, the Bible, in a deeper and more progressive way. By keeping our eyes on the Messiah through life's struggles, G-d will not only reveal His Word, the Bible, to us in a greater way, but He also will refine our faith like fine flour, just as was done to the wheat during the days of counting the *omer* between Passover (*Pesach*) and *Shavuot* (Pentecost). Meanwhile, if we put our entire trust (*emunah*) in *Yeshua* while on our spiritual journey in the wilderness of life as G-d refines our faith and reveals Himself to us in a greater way, then our spiritual journey will not end in the wilderness of life (Hallelujah!). Instead G-d will take us forward to spiritually experience the fall festivals and our spiritual promised land.

It is when we spiritually experience the fall festivals—especially the Feast of Tabernacles (*Sukkot*), *Shemini Atzeret* and *Simchat Torah*—and enter into our spiritual promised land that G-d will anoint our lives for Him in an awesome way, as we live and serve Him, and we will then experience the greatest joy in our entire lives. Joy unspeakable! But we will experience not only joy, but also dancing, praise, victory, peace, and the power of G-d in our lives. Spiritually, we will be experiencing the fall harvest of Israel. The rain in the Bible speaks of two things: the great outpouring of the Holy Spirit (*Ruach HaKodesh*) and an in-depth understanding of *Yeshua* and His Word, the Bible, in our lives. Both the anointing of the Holy Spirit (*Ruach HaKodesh*) and great knowledge of spiritual truths will be present in our lives in order that we may accomplish the purpose G-d has for every one of our lives. Therefore, we have the anointing of G-d upon our lives so we may help to do our part to build up the Body of Messiah to full maturity and to establish the Kingdom of G-d on earth until we come to that day when we will rule and reign with the Messiah, the King of kings and Lord of lords on earth during the Messianic age, the Millennium, and for all eternity.

Messianic Fulfillment and Understanding

When G-d created man and put him in the Garden of Eden (*Gan Eden*), the Garden of Eden was like paradise, Heaven, or the world to come, known in Hebrew as the *olam habba*. However, man sinned and as a result, both man and the earth was diminished in comparison to the original glory and beauty in which it was created. As a result, G-d laid out a 7,000-year plan to restore both man and the earth back to the glory and majesty of the Garden of Eden (*Gan Eden*). The Messiah was to play a central role in this redemption.

In Hosea 6:3 and Joel 2:23, the Scriptures tell us that the coming of the Messiah *Yeshua* will be like the rain. As previously discussed, in Israel there are the spring rains that are in the form of dew and showers, and the fall rains that make up the great rainy season. In His wisdom, G-d gave the weather season in Israel to teach about the coming of the Messiah. Just as there are mainly spring rains and fall rains in Israel, G-d designed for two comings of the Messiah. During the first coming of the Messiah, the Messiah would fulfill the role of Messiah ben Joseph, the suffering Messiah. During His second coming, the Messiah would fulfill the role of Messiah ben David, the King Messiah. Those who would receive the Messiah in the season of His first coming would, spiritually, be like the spring rains in Israel and G-d would pour out His Holy Spirit (*Ruach HaKodesh*) upon all people at this time. However, the greatest number of people who would accept the Messiah would be during the season of the fall rains in Israel, which speaks of the Messiah's second coming. The greatest outpouring of the Holy Spirit (*Ruach HaKodesh*) would be at this time as well.

This great outpouring of the Holy Spirit (*Ruach HaKodesh*) and the knowledge of the Messiah on earth will reach their greatest height during the Messianic age, the Millennium, and continuing into eternity. This is what the fall rains in Israel are spiritually all about and are why G-d instructed the people to pray for rain during the festival season of *Sukkot* including *Shemini Atzeret* and *Simchat Torah*. After all, *Sukkot* (Tabernacles) and *Shemini Atzeret* and *Simchat Torah* were given to us by G-d to instruct us what life would be like during the Messianic age and all eternity when the knowledge of the Messiah and the Spirit of G-d will cover the earth as the waters cover the sea, as prophesied in the Book of Zechariah. For *Yeshua* the Messiah is both the Former and Latter Rain and the Teacher of Righteousness (Hosea [*Hoshea*] 6:3; Joel [*Yoel*] 2:23; Psalm [*Tehillim*] 72:6; 84:5-6; John [*Yochanan*] 3:2; Isaiah [*Yeshayahu*] 55:10-12). How glorious it will be to live with the Messiah during those days! This is the essence of the festivals of the L-rd!

Chapter 11

Seventy Prophecies of *Yeshua's* First Coming[1]

1. **He would be a descendent of Abraham (*Avraham*).**
    (Genesis 12:1-3; 18:18; 22:18; Matthew 1:1-2,17; Galatians 3:8,16)

2. **He would be from the tribe of Judah (*Yehudah*).**
    (Genesis 49:8-10; Hebrews 7:14; Revelation 5:5)

3. **He would be a descendent of David.**
    (2 Samuel 7:4-5,12-13; 1 Chronicles 17:11-14; Psalm 132:11; Luke 1:32-33,67-69; Acts 2:29-30; Matthew 1:17; Romans 1:3)

4. **He would be born in Bethlehem (*Beit Lechem*).**
    (Micah 5:2; Matthew 2:4-6; John 7:42)

5. **He would be from Nazareth and be called a Nazarene.**
    (Matthew 2:23; Luke 1:26-27; John 1:45; Judges 13:5-7,24)

6. **The exact time of His crucifixion was known** (483 years from the decree to build the temple, which was

around 444 B.C.E.).
(Daniel 9:25; Nehemiah 2:1-8; 5:14)

7. **He would be born of a virgin.**
   (Isaiah 7:14; Matthew 1:20-23; Galatians 4:4; Genesis 3:15)

8. **His name would be Immanuel.** Immanuel in Hebrew means "G-d with us."
   (Isaiah 7:14; Matthew 1:21-23)

9. **His name would be Jesus (*Yeshua* in Hebrew), which means "Savior" or "Salvation."** The word *Yeshua* in Hebrew means "salvation." It is derived from another Hebrew word, *Yashah*, which means "to save, deliver, preserve, bring salvation, get victory." (Matthew 1:21)

10. **His name would be the Messiah.** The word *Christ* in English comes from the Greek word *Christos*, which means "The Anointed One." *Christos* in Greek is the word *Mashiach* in Hebrew, which also means "The Anointed One." The word *Mashiach* means "Messiah," who is *Yeshua.* (John 1:41)

11. **He would be the only begotten Son of G-d.**
    (Psalm 2:2,6-7; John 1:14; Acts 13:33; Hebrews 1:1-2,5)

12. **He would be the Son of G-d and G-d would be His Father.**
    (Psalm 89:26-27; 2 Samuel 7:8,12-14; 1 Chronicles 22:7-10; Hebrews 1:1-2,5; Mark 14:36; John 20:30-31)

13. **He would be circumcised the eighth day according to the law of purification.**
    (Luke 2:21-24; Leviticus 12:1-6)

14. **He would go to Egypt and return to the land of Israel.**
    (Hosea 11:1; Matthew 2:13-15)

15. **Young babies would die in an attempt to kill *Yeshua* at His birth.**
    (Jeremiah 31:15; Matthew 2:16-18)

16. **He would be preceded by a messenger (a type of Elijah [*Eliyahu*] known as John [*Yochanan*] the Immerser [Baptist]) who would prepare the way of the L-rd.**
    (Malachi 3:1; Luke 1:13,76; Matthew 11:7,10)

17. **The messenger, John (*Yochanan*) the Immerser (Baptist), would be preaching in the wilderness.**
    (Isaiah 40:3-5; Luke 1:13,80, 3:2-6)

18. **He would be a prophet like Moses (*Moshe*).**
    (Deuteronomy 18:15; John 1:45; Acts 3:20-23)

19. **He would be anointed of the Holy Spirit (*Ruach HaKodesh*).**
    (Isaiah 11:1-2; 42:1; Matthew 3:16)

20. **He would preach and teach in the temple (*Beit HaMikdash*).**
    (Malachi 3:1; Luke 4:16; Matthew 26:55; John 7:28; 8:1-2)

21. **He came specifically to the house of Israel and not to the Gentiles.** (Matthew 15:21-26)

22. ***Yeshua* would be rejected by His own people Israel (corporately).** [Note: It should be pointed out that many, many individual Jews were believers in Messiah during the first century. This can be seen very clearly by carefully examining Matthew, Mark,

Luke, John, and the Book of Acts. (Psalm 69:8; 31:11; 88:8,18; Job 19:13; John 1:11; 7:3,5)]
Yeshua is the stone that the builders rejected. (Psalm 118:22; Isaiah 3:10-12; Romans 9:11)

23. *Yeshua* **would be received by the Gentiles (corporately).** [Note: It should be pointed out that many Gentiles are not believers in *Yeshua* and many others are believers in name only and not true followers with their hearts. The believers in Messiah are commanded to follow G-d with all of their heart (Deuteronomy 6:4-9).]
(Isaiah 11:10; 42:6; 49:6,22; 54:3; 60:3,5,11,16; 61:6,9; 62:2; 66:12,19; Malachi 1:11; Luke 2:30-32; Acts 28:28)

24. **He would speak in parables.**
(Psalm 78:2-4; Matthew 13:34-35)

25. **The ministry of *Yeshua* would be in Galilee.**
(Isaiah 9:1-2; Matthew 4:12-16,23)

26. **His ministry would be to heal the sick, set the captives free, and preach deliverance.** This is known as the *basar* (gospel) in Hebrew.
(Isaiah 61:1-2; Luke 4:16-21; Matthew 4:23; 9:34-35; Acts 2:22; 10:38)

27. *Yeshua* **was to be the shepherd of Israel because Israel had no shepherd.**
(Ezekiel 34:5-10; 1 Kings 22:17; Zechariah 10:2; Genesis 49:22,24; Psalm 23:1; 80:1; Isaiah 40:10-11; Ezekiel 34:23-24; 37:24; John 10:11,14-15)

28. **His message would not be believed.**
(Isaiah 53:1; John 12:37-38)

29. **The meek would praise Him.**
    (Psalm 8:1-2; Matthew 21:15-16)

30. **Illegal merchandise trading would be done in the temple.**
    (Psalm 69:9; John 2:13-17; Isaiah 56:7; Matthew 21:12-13)

31. **He would be hated.**
    (Psalm 69:4; 35:19; 109:2-3; 119:161; John 15:24-25)

32. **He would be a reproach to the people.**
    (Psalm 69:9; 89:50-51; Romans 15:3)

33. **He would not seek publicity.**
    (Isaiah 42:1-2; Matthew 12:15-19; 9:30; 8:4)

34. **He can be trusted and would be compassionate.**
    (Isaiah 42:3; Matthew 12:15,20-21)

35. **No evil words would proceed from His mouth.**
    (Isaiah 53:9; Luke 23:41; 1 Peter 2:21-22; 2 Corinthians 5:21)

36. **His disciples would forsake Him.**
    (Zechariah 13:7; Matthew 26:31-35,56)

37. **There was nothing physically beautiful in Him to be desired.**
    (Isaiah 53:2; Psalm 22:6; Mark 6:1-3; Philippians 2:7)

38. **He gave up the glory in Heaven for the poverty of earth.**
    (Luke 9:58; 2 Corinthians 8:9)

39. **He would publicly enter Jerusalem (*Yerushalayim*) before the time of His crucifixion.**
    (Zechariah 9:9; Matthew 21:1-5)

40. **He would ride into Jerusalem (*Yerushalayim*) on a donkey.**
    (Zechariah 9:9; Matthew 21:5)

41. **He would be sold for 30 pieces of silver.**
    (Zechariah 11:12; Matthew 26:14-16)

42. **His betrayal price would be given for a potter's field.**
    (Zechariah 11:13; Matthew 27:3,7-10)

43. **He would be betrayed by a friend.**
    (Psalm 41:9; John 13:18-21)

44. **Both Jew and Gentile would conspire against Him.**
    (Psalm 2:1-2; Acts 4:27-28; Matthew 26:3; 27:1-2)

45. **He would be nailed to a tree.**
    (Deuteronomy 21:22-23; Psalm 22:16; John 19:18; 20:25)

46. **He would suffer for others.**
    (Isaiah 53:6; Matthew 20:28)

47. **He would die for our sins.**
    (Isaiah 53:5; 1 Corinthians 15:3; 1 Peter 2:24)

48. **He would be mocked.**
    (Psalm 22:7-8; Matthew 27:39-43)

49. **He would die with the transgressors.**
    (Isaiah 53:12; Mark 15:27-28)

50. **He would make intercession for His murderers.**
    (Isaiah 53:12; Luke 23:34)

51. **He would be smitten.**
    (Micah 5:1; Isaiah 50:6; Lamentations 3:30; Matthew 26:67; 27:30)

52. **He would be spit upon.**
(Isaiah 50:6; Matthew 26:67, 27:30)

53. **He would be forsaken by G-d.**
(Psalm 22:1; Matthew 27:46)

54. **He would be given gall and vinegar to eat and drink.**
(Psalm 69:21; Matthew 27:34,48)

55. **He opened not His mouth when accused.**
(Isaiah 53:7; Matthew 26:63-64; 27:12-14)

56. **His garments would be parted.**
(Psalm 22:18; Matthew 27:35)

57. **Not one bone would be broken.**
(Psalm 34:20; John 19:33,36)

58. **He would be pierced.**
(Zechariah 12:10; John 19:34,37)

59. **He would be like a lamb going to the slaughter.**
(Isaiah 53:7; Acts 8:26-35)

60. **He is King of the Jews (and the world).**
(Psalm 2:6; John 18:33,37; 19:19-22)

61. **He would be buried with the rich.**
(Isaiah 53:9; Matthew 27:57-60)

62. **He would die.**
(Isaiah 53:12; Matthew 27:50)

63. **His soul would not be left in hell.**
(Psalm 16:10; 49:15; 56:13; Acts 2:27,31; 13:33-35)

64. **He would rise from the dead.**
(Psalm 16:10; Luke 24:6,31,34; Acts 2:27-31; 13:35)

65. **Others would rise from the dead with Him.**
(Psalm 68:18; Ephesians 4:8; Matthew 27:52-53)

66. **He would rise the third day from the grave.**
    (Jonah 1:17; 1 Corinthians 15:4; Luke 24:45-46; Matthew 12:40)

67. **He would ascend into Heaven.**
    (Psalm 68:18; Acts 1:9; Luke 24:50-51)

68. **He would sit at the right hand of G-d.**
    (Psalm 110:1; Hebrews 1:2-3; Ephesians 1:20-21; 1 Peter 3:22)

69. **He would usher in a New Covenant (*Brit Hadashah*).**
    (Jeremiah 31:31; Luke 22:20)

70. **He would be a sure foundation to all who believe.**
    (Isaiah 28:16; Romans 10:11; 1 Peter 2:4-6)

Chapter 12

How Can I Receive the Messiah Into My Heart and Life?

The G-d of Abraham, Isaac, and Jacob created you to have a *personal relationship* with Himself and to *enjoy His abundant life*! In Proverbs 16:4 [it is written in the Jewish Bible] "The Lord has made all things for His purpose [His own pleasure]." In Psalm 16:11 it is written, "...At Thy right hand there are *pleasures* for *evermore*."

Sin (the transgression or *breaking* of G-d's law) *separates* you from a personal relationship with G-d and His abundant life. *Sin also causes spiritual death!* In Isaiah 59:2a it is written, "But your iniquities [your sins] have *separated* between *you* and *your G-d*." Man was created to have fellowship with G-d, but stubbornly chose to go his own independent way. This *self-will* (expressed by either *active rebellion* or *passive indifference* toward G-d) is what the Bible calls "sin." Sin separates you from G-d and causes spiritual death, guilt, lack of peace, frustration, etc. In Ezekiel (*Yechezekel*) 18:4 it is written, "...the *soul* that sinneth, it shall *die* [spiritual death]." In First Kings (*Melachim*) 8:46 it is written, "...for there is *no* man that *sinneth not*."

You cannot remove sin by your *own human* efforts. In Isaiah 64:5 it is written, "...all *our* righteousnesses [our self-righteousness] are as *filthy rags*...." In Proverbs 14:12 it is written, "There is a way which *seemeth* right unto a man, but the *end* thereof are the ways of *death* [spiritual *separation* from G-d]." Man's plan is to *remove* his *own sin* by his *own self-righteousness* (i.e., to outweigh his *bad deeds* by his *"good" deeds*, such as religious *"works," human philosophies*, etc.). Man's *self-righteousness* is a *"filthy garment"* in the sight of a *holy* G-d.

Sin *can* be removed by *faith* (*emunah*, *believing* what *G-d* says). Righteousness (right standing with G-d) comes by faith. In Genesis (*Bereishit*) 15:6 it is written, "And he [Abraham] *believed* [had faith] in the L-rd; and He counted it [Abraham's faith] to him for *righteousness*." *Faith must be placed in the blood atonement.* Atonement means a "covering" for sin. In Leviticus (*Vayikra*) 17:11 it is written, "...for it is the *blood* that maketh an *atonement* [covering] for the *soul*."

G-d has provided the blood of atonement today through a *perfect sacrifice*: the One who is known as the Messiah. Messiah means "anointed" one. In Isaiah 53:5 it is written, "But *He* was wounded for our transgressions [rebellions], *He* was bruised for our iniquities [moral evils]: the chastisement [punishment] of our peace [welfare] was upon *Him*; and with *His* stripes [wounds, *blood*] we were healed [*atoned for*]." In Abel we see atonement for a *man* as it is written in Genesis (*Bereishit*) 4:4, "And Abel, he also brought of the firstlings of his flock...." During Passover, we saw an atonement for a *family*, as it is written in Exodus 12:13, "...when I see the *blood*, I will *pass over* you…." During *Yom Kippur*, we see atonement for a *nation*, as it is written in Leviticus 16:30a, "For on *that day* shall the priest make *an atonement* for you." The Messiah brings atonement for *all who believe*, as it is written in Isaiah 53:6. "But the Lord has caused the iniquity [the sins] of us *all* to *fall* [to focus] on *Him*."

How can you know the Messiah *Yeshua*? You must *ask* the Messiah *Yeshua into your heart and life* in order to have the blood of atonement, to have a personal relationship with G-d, and to enjoy His abundant life (the Messiah will not force His way into your life; He *desires* to be *invited*). In Joel 3:5 it is written, "…whosoever shall *call* on the *name* of the *Lord* shall be delivered [*saved*]…." If you are desiring to ask the Messiah *Yeshua* into your heart and life, you may do so by following these simple steps.

1. Pray to G-d in your own words (prayer is just *talking* to G-d).
2. Confess that you have sinned against G-d and that you are truly sorry for it.
3. Ask the Messiah *Yeshua* into your heart and life to cleanse you with His blood of atonement.
4. Thank Him by *faith* for doing this!

The following is a sample prayer which you might pray.

"Dear G-d, I confess that I have greatly sinned against You and I'm sorry for it. Messiah *Yeshua*, please come into my heart and life and cleanse me with Your blood of atonement. Thank You for doing this *according to Your Word*."

If you have prayed this prayer and mean it, G-d has promised you many wonderful things, including the following:

1. Your sins are *atoned* for (covered, forgiven) (Isaiah 53:6).
2. You receive *righteousness* (right-standing with G-d) by *faith* (Genesis 15:6; Habakkuk 2:4).
3. You enter into a *personal relationship with G-d* and you become a *child of G-d* (Jeremiah 31:32).
4. You receive *eternal life* (Joel 3:5; Daniel 12:2).
5. G-d's *Holy Spirit* (*Ruach HaKodesh*) *enters your life* (Ezekiel 11:19; Zechariah 12:10)![1]

If you have made a decision to accept the Messiah into your life and you are Jewish, congratulations! Continue to be Jewish and please try to find a local Messianic synagogue to attend, for you have just became a completed Jew. If you are non-Jewish and have made a decision to accept the Messiah *Yeshua* into your life, please find a local Bible-believing church to attend or a Messianic synagogue.

Regardless of whether you are Jewish or non-Jewish, if you have made a decision to accept the Messiah *Yeshua* into your life, I would like to hear from you. In addition, if you would like to obtain further Messianic material or training, or if this book has been a blessing to you in any way, please write me at the following address:

The Seven Festivals of the Messiah
P.O. Box 81
Strasburg, Ohio 44680

G-d bless you as you seek to grow in the knowledge of the Messiah!

ENJOY THE *FESTIVALS* BOOK?

Edward Chumney has written
TWO other books!!

WHO IS THE BRIDE OF CHRIST?
and
RESTORING THE TWO HOUSES OF ISRAEL

ORDER TODAY!!!

I pray that this book, *The Seven Festivals of the Messiah*, has been a source of inspiration and rich blessing to you. If it has, I would encourage you to read the two other books that I have written. They are entitled: *Who Is the Bride of Christ?* and *Restoring the Two Houses of Israel*.

The book, *Who Is the Bride of Christ?*, is a study of the biblical characteristics of the Bride of Messiah. It also shows how the future role and destiny of the Bride of Messiah in the Kingdom of G-d is related and associated with embracing our rich Hebraic heritage in Messiah. This book is $12.00 (USD), postage paid.

The book, *Restoring the Two Houses of Israel*, is a study of why there has been a historical division between Christianity and Judaism and how they will be reunited in Messiah in the end of days. In examining the historical division between Christianity and Judaism, the book has chapters on the subject of the Sabbath, Torah and Grace, the 7,000-year plan of the G-d of Israel, the Jewishness of the Messiah and the issue of the Messiah being the G-d of Israel manifested in the flesh. In examining the restoration and reunification of both the houses of Israel in the end of days and their return to the land of Israel prior to the coming of King Messiah to rule and reign during the Messianic Era, the book has chapters on the history of the modern-day state of Israel, the importance of Jerusalem, the judgment of the nations and how the current Israel/Arab peace process based upon U.N. Resolutions 242 and 338 will eventually set in motion events that will culminate in the restoration and reunification of both houses of Israel and the coming of King Messiah. This book is $12.00 (USD), postage paid.

If you order *Who Is the Bride of Christ?* and *Restoring the Two Houses of Israel*, the cost is $25.00 (USD), postage paid, for both books. Please send all orders to *Hebraic Heritage Ministries International* address given on the next page.

Volume discounts from 40% - 50% are available for this book, *The Seven Festivals of the Messiah*, and for my other two books *Who Is the Bride of Christ?* and *Restoring the Two Houses of Israel* when you order six or more copies of the Bride book, or six or more copies of the Two Houses of Israel book. If you are interested in this offer, please send me an e-mail at chumney@hebroots.org for more detailed information.

If you have a greater interest in studying the Hebraic roots of faith in the Jewish Messiah (*Mashiach*) *Yeshua*/Jesus, I would encourage you to visit the *Hebraic Heritage Ministries International* website and join the global network of ministries and individuals who are doing so by filling out the ministry guest book located at the website. Furthermore, at the website you will find *many* articles that will help you in studying the Hebraic roots of faith in Messiah. For more information about *Hebraic Heritage Ministries International*, please see the following page.

HEBRAIC HERITAGE
MINISTRIES INTERNATIONAL

- Teaching the Hebraic roots of faith in Messiah.

- Networking groups who are studying the Hebraic roots of faith in Messiah.

- Standing with the Jewish people and fighting anti-Semitism.

- Christian Zionists who have a loving heart for the land of Israel.

Please visit our website and join our network!

www.geocities.com/Heartland/2175/index.html

OR

www.hebroots.org

Mailing Address:

Hebraic Heritage Ministries International
P.O. Box 81
Strasburg, Ohio, USA 44680

Endnotes

Chapter 1—The Appointed Feasts

1.   Adapted from Kevin J. Conner's *The Feasts of Israel*, (Portland, Oregon: Bible Temple Publishing, 1980), p. 1.

2.   James Strong, *The Exhaustive Concordance of the Bible*, (Peabody, Massachusetts: Hendrickson Pub. n.d.), definition #4150.

3.   Strong's, #2282.

4.   Strong's, #2287.

Chapter 2—An Overview of the Festivals

1.   Strong's, #4175.

2.   Strong's, #6666.

3.   Strong's, #4744.

Chapter 3—Passover (*Pesach*): Feasting for Freedom

1.   Adapted from Conner's *The Feasts of Israel*, pp. 16-22.

2.   Joseph Good, "Rosh HaShanah and the Messianic Kingdom to Come," (tape series) (Port Arthur, Texas: Hatikva Ministries, 1989). Tape #3, "The Festivals."

3.   Adapted from Conner's *The Feasts of Israel*, pp. 85-86.

Chapter 4—The Festival of Unleavened Bread (*Hag HaMatzah*)

1.   Good, "Rosh HaShanah and the Messianic Kingdom to Come." Tape #4, "Pesach to Shavuot."

2.   Adapted from Grant R. Jeffrey's *Armageddon Appointment with Destiny*, (Toronto, Ontario: Frontier Research Publications, 1988), p. 58.

3.   Good, "Rosh HaShanah and the Messianic Kingdom to Come." Tape #4, "Pesach to Shavuot."

4.   Adapted from Conner's *The Feasts of Israel,* pp. 24-25.

Chapter 5—The Festival of First Fruits (*Bikkurim*)

1.   Adapted from Conner's *The Feasts of Israel*, p. 29.

2.   Ibid.

3.   Adapted from Jeffrey's *Armageddon Appointment with Destiny*, p. 60.

4.   Joseph Good, "The Festival Series I," (tape series) (Port Arthur, Texas: Hatikva Ministries). Tape #3, "Overview: The Seven Festivals."

5.   Adapted from Conner's *The Feasts of Israel*, p. 30.

6. Good, "Rosh HaShanah and the Messianic Kingdom to Come." Tape #3, "The Festivals."

Chapter 6—The Festival of Pentecost (*Shavuot*)

1. Adapted from Michael Strassfeld, *The Jewish Holidays: A Guide and Commentary* (New York, New York: Harper and Row, 1985), pp. 47-49.

2. Ibid.

3. Adapted from Isador Margolis and Rabbi Sidney L. Markowitz, *The Jewish Holidays and Festivals* (New York, New York: Carol Publishing Group, 1962), pp. 44-45.

4. Strassfeld, *The Jewish Holidays*, p. 71.

5. Adapted from Jeffrey's *Armageddon Appointment with Destiny*, pp. 65-67.

6. Strassfeld, *The Jewish Holidays*, p. 75.

7. Adapted from Rabbi Aryeh Kaplan, *Made in Heaven* (Brooklyn, New York: Moznaim Publishing Corporation, 1983), p. 134.

8. Ibid.

9. Strassfeld, *The Jewish Holidays*, p. 113.

10. Ibid., p. 75.

11. Adapted from Rabbi Moshe Weissman, *The Midrash Says on Shemot* (Brooklyn, New York: Benei Yakov Publications, 1980), p. 82.

12. Good, "Rosh HaShanah and the Messianic Kingdom to Come." Tape #4, "The Two Calendars."

13. Adapted from Conner's *The Feasts of Israel*, pp. 38-42.

Chapter 7—*Rosh HaShanah*

1. Good, "Rosh HaShanah and the Messianic Kingdom to Come." Tape #7, "Teshuvah."

2. Strassfeld, *The Jewish Holidays*, p. 97.

3. Good, "Rosh HaShanah and the Messianic Kingdom to Come." Tape #7, "Teshuvah."

4. Ibid.

5. Adapted from Mitch and Zhava Glaser's, *The Fall Feasts of Israel*, (Chicago, Illinois: Moody Press, 1987), pp. 22-23.

6. Strassfeld, *The Jewish Holidays*, p. 28.

7. Adapted from Margolis and Markowitz, *The Jewish Holidays and Festivals*, p. 28.

8. Adapted from Nissan Mindel, *The Complete Story of Tishrei* (Brooklyn, New York: Mekkos L'inyonei Chinuch Inc., 1956), p. 18.

9. Strassfeld, *The Jewish Holidays*, pp. 102-103.

10. Ibid., p. 96.

11. Mindel, *The Complete Story of Tishrei*, p. 47.

12. Strassfeld, *The Jewish Holidays*, p. 100.

13. Good, "Rosh HaShanah and the Messianic Kingdom to Come." Tape #6, "Yom Teruah."

14. Ibid.

15. Mindel, *The Complete Story of Tishrei*, p. 47.

16. Adapted from Louis E. Kaplan, *The Gates of Mercy* (New York, New York: Sepher-Hermon Press, 1979), p. 40.

17. *Gates of Repentance*, p. 139, as quoted in Central Conference of American Rabbis, *Gates of the Seasons* (New York, 1983), p. 120.

18. Good, "Rosh HaShanah and the Messianic Kingdom to Come." Tape #6, "Yom Teruah."

19. Good, "Rosh HaShanah and the Messianic Kingdom to Come." Tape #7, "Teshuvah."

20. Good, "Rosh HaShanah and the Messianic Kingdom to Come." Tape #6, "Yom Teruah."

21. Glaser, *The Fall Feasts of Israel*, pp. 22-23.

22. Good, "Rosh HaShanah and the Messianic Kingdom to Come." Tape #7, "Teshuvah."

23. Mindel, *The Complete Story of Tishrei*, p. 19.

24. Ibid., pp. 22-23.

25. Good, "Rosh HaShanah and the Messianic Kingdom to Come." Tape #11, "The Coronation."

26. Adapted from Margolis and Markowitz, *The Jewish Holidays and Festivals*, p. 31.

27. Good, "Rosh HaShanah and the Messianic Kingdom to Come." Tape #6, "Yom Teruah."

28. Good, "Rosh HaShanah and the Messianic Kingdom to Come." Tape #4, "The Two Calendars."

29.   Adapted from Central Conference of American Rabbis, *Gates of the Season*, p. 39.

30.   Adapted from Neil and Jamie Lash's "Ancient Jewish Wedding Customs," (tape series) (Ft. Lauderdale, Florida: Love Song to the Messiah Association).

31.   Good, "Rosh HaShanah and the Messianic Kingdom to Come." Tape #11, "Natzal and the Resurrection."

32.   Adapted from Mindel, *The Complete Story of Tishrei*, p. 19.

33.   Ibid.

34.   Good, "Rosh HaShanah and the Messianic Kingdom to Come." Tape #12, "The Wedding."

Chapter 8—*Yom Kippur*: The Day of Atonement

1.   Adapted from Arthur Waskow's *Seasons of Our Joy* (New York, New York: Bantam Books, 1982), pp. 28-29.

2.   Glaser, *The Fall Feasts of Israel*, p. 88.

3.   Ibid., p. 104.

4.   Ibid., p. 85.

5.   Adapted from Waskow's, *Seasons of Our Joy*, p. 29.

6.   Good, "Rosh HaShanah and the Messianic Kingdom to Come." Tape #5, "The 7,000-Year Plan of God."

7.   Adapted from Margolis and Markowitz, *The Jewish Holidays and Festivals*, p. 37.

8. Adapted from Central Conference of American Rabbis, *Gates of the Seasons*, p. 49.

9. Adapted from Margolis and Markowitz, *The Jewish Holidays and Festivals*, p. 39.

10. Adapted from Central Conference of American Rabbis, *Gates of the Seasons*, p. 50.

11. Adapted from Conner's *The Feasts of Israel*, pp. 53-58.

12. Adapted from Glaser, *The Fall Feasts of Israel*, pp. 79-80.

13. Ibid., pp. 81-82.

14. Good, "Rosh HaShanah and the Messianic Kingdom to Come." Tape #5, "The 7,000-Year Plan of God."

15. Good, "The Festival Series I." Tape #5, "The High Holy Days."

Chapter 9—*Sukkot*: The Feast of Tabernacles

1. Adapted from Strassfeld's, *The Jewish Holidays*, p. 125.

2. Central Conference of American Rabbis, *The Gates of the Seasons*, p. 80.

3. Adapted from Strassfeld's, *The Jewish Holidays*, p. 145.

4. Adapted from Mindel's, *The Complete Story of Tishrei*, p. 143.

5. Glaser, *The Fall Feasts of Israel*, p. 155.

6. Adapted from Conner's *The Feasts of Israel*, p. 69.

7.   Strassfeld, *The Jewish Holidays*, p. 125.

8.   Mindel, *The Complete Story of Tishrei*, p. 147.

9.   Central Conference of American Rabbis, *Gates of the Seasons*, p. 80.

10.   Strassfeld, *The Jewish Holidays*, p. 129.

11.   Adapted from Conner's *The Feasts of Israel*, pp. 205-206.

12.   Strassfeld, *The Jewish Holidays*, p. 129.

13.   Ibid.

14.   Adapted from Waskow's, *Seasons of Our Joy,* p. 50.

15.   Margolis and Markowitz, *The Jewish Holidays and Festivals*, pp. 44-45.

16.   Adapted from Waskow's, *Season of our Joy*, p. 51.

17.   Adapted from Strassfeld's, *The Jewish Holidays*, p. 135.

18.   Waskow, *Seasons of Our Joy*, p. 51.

19.   Good, "Rosh HaShanah and the Messianic Kingdom to Come." Tape #5, "The 7,000-Year Plan of God."

20.   Glaser, *The Fall Feasts of Israel*, p. 174.

21.   Ibid., p. 176.

22.   Strassfeld, *The Jewish Holidays*, p. 135.

23.   Glaser, *The Fall Feasts of Israel*, pp. 179-180, 185.

24. Ibid., pp. 182-183.

25. Adapted from Good's "Rosh HaShanah and the Messianic Kingdom to Come," Appendix I, "The Birth of Yeshua during Sukkot", and from *The Gates*, "The Birth of Yeshua during Sukkot," (Port Arthur, Texas: Hatikva Ministries), Fall 1992.

26. Ibid.

27. Ibid.

Chapter 10—*Shemini Atzeret* and *Simchat Torah*

1. Strassfeld, *The Jewish Holidays*, p. 149.

2. Ibid.

3. Ibid., p. 158.

4. Ibid., p. 149.

5. Ibid., p. 158.

6. Mindel, *The Complete Story of Tishrei*, p. 176.

7. Adapted from Margolis and Markowitz's *The Jewish Holidays and Festivals*, p. 46.

8. Adapted from Mindel's, *The Complete Story of Tishrei*, p. 192.

9. Strassfeld, *The Jewish Holidays*, p. 150.

10. Ibid., p. 150.

11. Adapted from Mindel's, *The Complete Story of Tishrei*, pp. 177-178.

Chapter 11—Seventy Prophecies of *Yeshua's* First Coming

1.   Adapted from "The Messianic Prophecy Card" (Bethesda, Maryland: The Messianic Jewish Movement International).

Chapter 12—How Can I Receive the Messiah Into My Heart and Life?

1.   Adapted from *Have You Ever Heard of the Five Jewish Laws?* by Manny Brotman, President, The Messianic Jewish Movement International, Inc., Bethesda, Maryland, © 1974, 1994.

Bibliography

"Birth of Yeshua during Sukkot, The," *The Gates*. Port Arthur, Texas: Hatikva Ministries, Fall 1992.

Central Conference of American Rabbis. *Gates of the Seasons*. New York, 1983.

Conner, Kevin J. *The Feasts of Israel*. Portland, Oregon: Bible Temple Publications, 1980.

Gastor, Theodor. *Festivals of the Jewish Year*. New York: William Morrow Co., 1952.

Glaser, Mitch and Zhava. *The Fall Feasts of Israel*. Chicago, Illinois: Moody Press, 1987.

Good, Joseph. "The Festival Series I." Port Arthur, Texas: Hatikva Ministries.

Good, Joseph. "Rosh HaShanah and the Messianic Kingdom to Come." Port Arthur, Texas: Hatikva Ministries, 1989.

"Have You Ever Heard of the Five Jewish Laws." Bethesda, Maryland: The Messianic Jewish Movement International, 1974.

Jeffrey, Grant R. *Armageddon Appointment with Destiny.* Toronto, Ontario: Frontier Research Publications, 1988.

Kaplan, Rabbi Aryeh. *Made in Heaven, A Jewish Wedding Guide.* New York: Moznaim Publishing, 1983.

Kaplan, Louis E. *The Gates of Mercy.* New York: Sepher-Hermon Press, 1979.

Kieval, Herman. *The High Holy Days.* New York: The Burning Bush Press, 1959.

Lash, Neil and Jamie. "Ancient Jewish Wedding Customs." Ft. Lauderdale, Florida: Love Song to the Messiah Association.

Margolis, Isador, and Markowitz, Rabbi Sydney L. *The Jewish Holidays and Festivals.* New York, New York: Carol Publishing Group, 1962.

"The Messianic Prophecy Card." Bethesda, Maryland: The Messianic Jewish Movement International.

Mindel, Nissan. *The Complete Story of Tishrei.* Brooklyn, New York: Makkos L'inyonei Chinuch, Inc., 1956.

Strassfeld, Michael. *The Jewish Holidays: A Guide and Commentary.* New York: Harper and Row Publications, 1985.

Strong, James. *Exhaustive Concordance of the Bible.* Peabody, Massachusetts: World Bible Publishers, 1980.

Waskow, Arthur. *Seasons of Our Joy*. New York: Bantam Books, 1982.

Weissman, Rabbi Moshe. *The Midrash Says*. Vols. 1-5. Brooklyn, New York: Benei Yakov Publications, 1980.

Glossary of Terms

Abib
Original name of the first biblical calendar month Nisan.

Afikomen
Name of the middle *matzah* of the three *matzot* on the Passover plate. It is eaten at the conclusion of the Seder meal. This is a Greek word meaning "that which comes after." It is represented in a broken piece of *matzah* wrapped in linen and buried (hidden).

Arba Minim
"Four species." These are the four species gathered during the *Sukkot* festival: citron (*etrog*), palm (*lulav*), myrtle (*hadas*), and willow (*aravah*).

Atzeret
A festive gathering for the conclusion of a festive season; a concluding feast. The eighth day of *Sukkot* known as *Shemini Atzeret*.

Azazel   Name of the goat (scapegoat) driven into the wilderness in the temple service for *Yom Kippur*.

Bedikat Chamets   "Search for *Chamets* (leavened bread)." A symbolic search for the last remains of leaven conducted on the night before the first Passover Seder.

Beit HaMikdash   The sanctuary of the temple in Jerusalem.

Beit HaShoevah   The house of the water pouring. This is associated with a water pouring celebration and ceremony that is done during the festival of *Sukkot*.

Beit Din   A rabbinic court.

Bikkurim   "First Fruits." In ancient times, this involved bringing the first seasonal fruits to the temple in Jerusalem.

Chametz   "Leaven." Leaven products are not to be eaten during Passover. Leaven is symbolic of sin.

Chupah   The marriage canopy under which the bride and groom stand to be married.

Elul   Sixth month on the biblical calendar. Elul 1 begins a 40-day period of repentance that concludes on *Yom Kippur*. This 40-day period is known as *Teshuvah*.

Erusin   Betrothal. The first of two steps of a biblical wedding.

Get   A divorce document.

Hag   Holiday, festival.

Hag HaMatzah   "The Festival of Unleavened Bread." This is during the season of Passover.

Hakkafah   Circle-dance (one circuit) with the Torah scroll.

Ha Melech   "The King." The coronation day of the Messiah. The same as *Rosh HaShanah*.

Hoshanah   Hebrew word meaning "save now." This is said while carrying the Torah in a procession.

Hoshana Rabbah   The seventh day of *Sukkot*, known as the "Great Hosanna."

Karpas   "Parsley, green herbs." One of the items on the Passover plate.

Ketubah   A written marriage contract.

Lulav   "Palm branch." The willow, myrtle, and palm branches are bound together and waved in rejoicing during *Sukkot*.

Maror	"Bitter herbs." One of the items of the Passover Seder plate.
Mashiach	"The Anointed One." The Hebrew word for Messiah, or Christ.
Matan Torah	"The giving of the Torah." The revelation on Mount Sinai.
Matzah	Unleavened bread eaten during Passover and especially at the Seder.
Messianic	Having to do with the Messiah (*Yeshua*, Jesus).
Miqra	Convocation, a rehearsal.
Mishnah	The first legal law code of basic Jewish law governing all aspects of life. It is based upon the Pharisees' and rabbis' interpretation of the Torah and was arranged and reenacted by R. Judah Hanasi about 200 C.E. The Mishnah contains the basic oral law as evolved through the generations. It is divided into six orders.
Mo'ed	A set time or appointed time. Season; festival.
Natzal	"Deliverance." Used to denote the catching away of the believers in the Messiah at the start of the last thousand years of the Messianic era.

Neilah   "Conclusion, closing." The closing of the gates service at the end of *Yom Kippur*.

Nisan   The first month of the biblical calendar. This is the religious calendar order given by G-d in Exodus 12.

Omer   "Sheaf; wave offering." A bushel of grain. The counting of the *omer* refers to the period between Passover and *Shavuot*.

Pentecost   English name given for the Feast of Weeks (*Shavuot*). This is the fiftieth day after the sabbath during Passover.

Pesach   "Passover." Historically, it commemorates the Israelites' exodus from Egypt, with the concept of freedom as its main theme.

Rosh Chodesh "The new moon, the new month." The first day of the month.

Rosh HaShanah The Jewish new year. Celebrated on the first day of Tishrei. The biblical name for *Rosh HaShanah* is *Yom Teruah*, which means "the day of the awakening blast." It is known in the non-Jewish world as the Feast of Trumpets.

Seder	Set order or arrangement. This refers to the Passover meal.
Shemini Atzeret	The eighth day of the Feast of *Sukkot*.
Shavuot	"Weeks." Known in English as Pentecost. *Shavuot* is the beginning of the wheat harvest, the season of the giving of the Torah, and also the time of betrothal between Israel and G-d.
Shitre Erusin	A betrothal contract.
Shofar	A trumpet made from a ram's horn.
Simchat Torah	"Rejoicing in the Torah." The festival marking the annual completion and recommencing of the Torah reading cycle. *Simchat Torah* is the first day following the festival season of *Sukkot*.
Sukkah	"Booth." A temporary shelter used during the festival of *Sukkot*, woven together from branches and leaves.
Sukkot	"Booths, tabernacles." The fall harvest festival, which goes from the fifteenth through the twenty-first of Tishrei.
Talmud	"Study or learning." The body of teaching that comprises the commentary and

discussions of the early rabbis on the Mishnah of R. Judah Hanasi. The Talmud is the code of Jewish law that is composed of the Mishnah and the Gemara. The Talmud has unparalleled influence on Jewish thought and is the foundation for modern day traditional Judaism.

Teshuvah "Repent or return." Repentance denoting a return to G-d after sin. Starts on Elul 1 through Tishrei 10.

Torah "Teaching or instruction." Used primarily to denote five books of the Bible.

Tzaddikim The righteous people (by *emunah* in G-d).

Ushpizin "Guests." According to tradition, the seven mystical "guests" (Abraham, Isaac, Jacob, Moses, Aaron, Joseph, and David) who visit the *Sukkah* during *Sukkot*.

Yamim Nora'im "Days of Awe." The period of days between *Rosh HaShanah* and *Yom Kippur*.

Yeshua Hebrew name meaning "salvation." The English word for *Yeshua* is Jesus.

Yom Hebrew word for "day."

Yom HaDin   "Day of Judgment." The same as *Rosh HaShanah*.

Yom Kippur   "Day of Atonement." A solemn day of fasting and prayer concluding the ten days of repentance that began on *Rosh HaShanah*. *Yom Kippur* is the tenth day of Tishrei.

Yom Teruah   "Day of Blowing, Awakening Blast, or Sounding the Shofar." The same as *Rosh HaShanah*.

Zeroah   "Arm." A roasted shankbone burned or scorched, which is one of the items of the Seder plate.

Additional copies of this book and other
book titles from DESTINY IMAGE are
available at your local bookstore.

For a complete list of our titles,
visit us at www.destinyimage.com
Send a request for a catalog to:

Destiny Image₍ Publishers, Inc.

P.O. Box 310
Shippensburg, PA 17257-0310

*"Speaking to the Purposes of God for This
Generation and for the Generations to Come"*